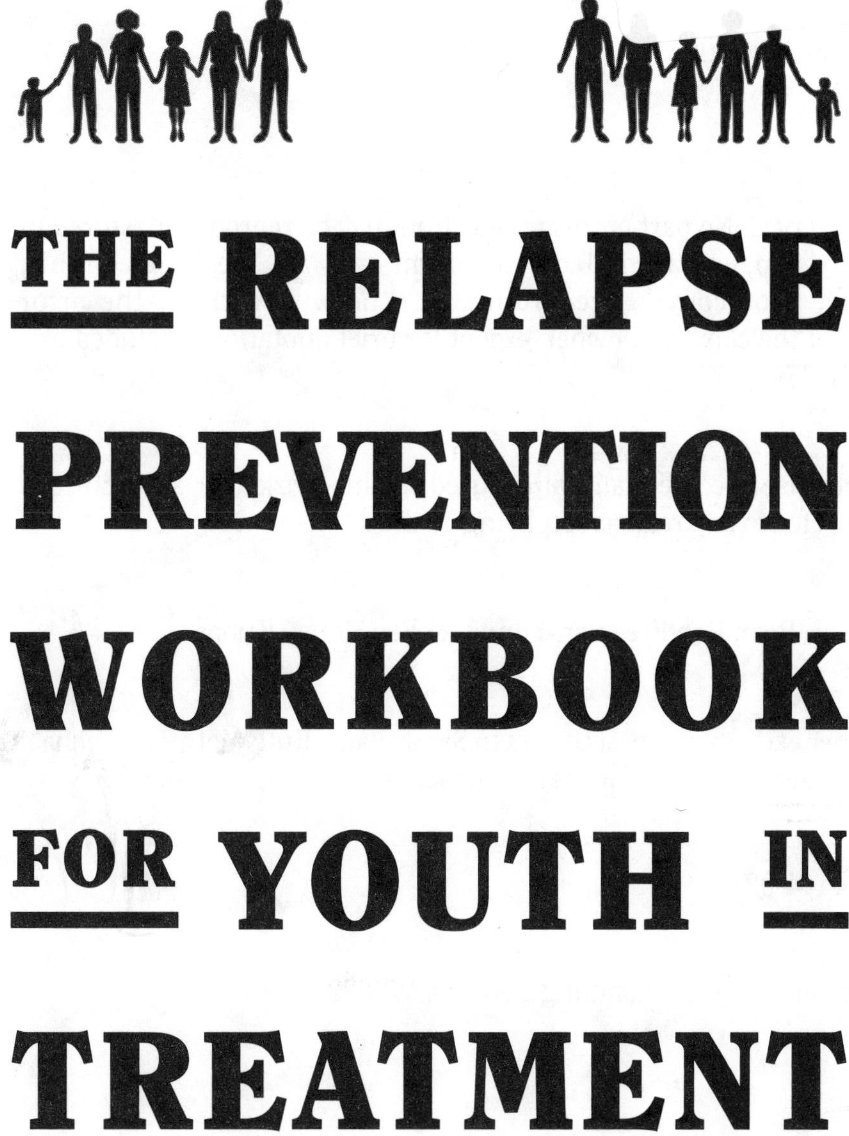

THE RELAPSE PREVENTION WORKBOOK FOR YOUTH IN TREATMENT

CHARLENE STEEN

The Safer Society Press
P.O. Box 340   Brandon, Vermont 05733-0340

Eleventh Printing 2006

Editors: Euan Bear, Rob Freeman-Longo, & Fay Honey Knopp

The publisher extends warmest thanks to Sandy Lane, Ruth Mathews, Michael O'Brien, and Jerry Thomas for their feedback on this manuscript.

ISBN 1-884444-02-4

$18.00 Plus shipping and handling / order # WP022

Order from:

A program of the Safer Society Foundation, Inc

(802) 247-3132 tel / (802) 247-4233 fax
Phone orders welcome with Visa or MasterCard
Bulk discounts available, please call for information.
www.safersociety.org

ALL ORDERS MUST BE PREPAID, U.S. FUNDS ONLY

Also avaliable:

Pathways: A Guided Workbook for Youth Beginning Treatment

CONTENTS

LIST OF EXERCISES

CHAPTER ONE

INTRODUCTION TO RELAPSE PREVENTION

You are in a treatment program due to some type of inappropriate or harmful sexual activity. You probably would prefer to be somewhere else, but have been required to participate. You must be wondering why you have to be here and what this treatment stuff is all about.

"Why do I need treatment? I'll never commit a sex offense again. I've learned my lesson." Your therapist has heard statements like this many times. Yet history has taught that many younger people who have behaved like you have often do reoffend, sometimes soon after and sometimes many years later, *if they haven't had treatment.* In addition, the offenses they commit usually worsen or become more frequent as time goes on. Many male adult offenders in prison began offending as children and never had the opportunity to participate in a sex offender treatment program. You don't want that to happen to you. You want to be as sure as you can be that you will never commit a sex offense again. Your job now is to learn how to keep from ever committing a sex offense again.

That is why this workbook was written. It was designed to help *you* help *yourself.* Relapse Prevention is a fancy way of saying "I'll never slip back into sex offending behavior again." You can think of it as a kind of insurance policy against reoffending. It gives you the power to prevent your own sex offending behavior in the future.

"So, what's it all about?" you ask. That is what this book will explain to you. The exercises in this book will give you more understanding of yourself and your behavior and help you to stop yourself *before* you reoffend.

Now for an explanation of **Relapse Prevention**. *Relapse* simply means committing another sex offense. And you know what *prevention* means. It means stopping it *before* it happens. In order to stop it, it is important to know how it starts. It's like a chain reaction: let's call it a reoffense chain. The Reoffense Chain on the next page shows how you can go from a Seemingly Unimportant Decision – let's call that a "SUD" – to an offense. It shows how a simple little act can get the whole thing started.

And now for an explanation of what these things mean.....

Abstinence (Not Offending) means what it says. You are not committing any offenses and you are not planning to commit any. This does not mean abstaining from *healthy* sexual behaviors.

SUDs (Seemingly Unimportant Decisions) are the everyday decisions you make that are reasonable-*looking,* but are risky because they have the possibility of placing you in a situation where you might offend. For example, let's consider the case of Bill. Bill had previously molested a child. He is home alone watching TV. A neighbor comes to the door. She is frantic. Her baby has cut off his finger in the door and she must take him to the hospital immediately. She asks Bill if he will watch her 5-year-old child while she goes.

On the surface, saying, "Yes, of course," sounds like a reasonable choice for Bill to make. But it isn't, because it places Bill in a high-risk and dangerous situation – on the first rung toward reoffense. It doesn't mean Bill is going to reoffend, but reoffense is more possible.

Dangerous Situation is just what it says – dangerous. It is dangerous because it places Bill in a situation where he has the opportunity to offend. The child is there alone with Bill. There is no one to stop Bill if he wants to offend. Again, it doesn't mean Bill is *going* to reoffend. However, he is much closer to reoffending because he is in a place where it is possible to offend.

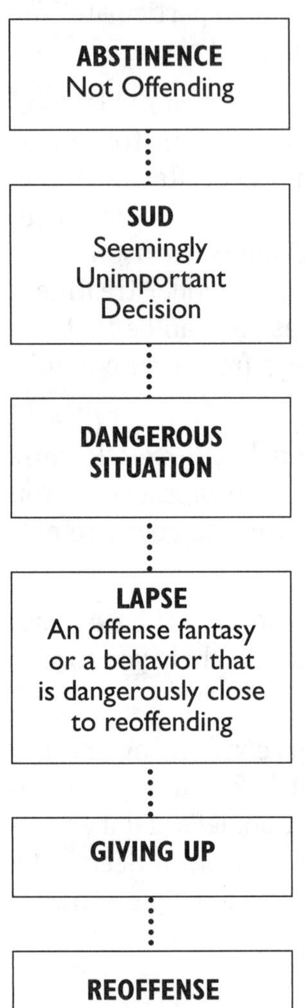

Lapse is either 1) a *behavior* that brings you very close to a sex offense, or 2) a *fantasy or daydream of committing a sex offense.* For example, in Bill's situation, perhaps the child starts climbing on him. He sits the child down on his lap and places his hand on the child's thigh to keep him from wiggling around. The act of putting his hand on the child's thigh can be defined as a lapse. It isn't a sex offense, but it gets very close to one. Bill should not be touching a child's thigh even for non-sexual reasons. He is on the edge of committing a sexual offense. It is much easier to commit an offense when you are in such a risky situation.

Another kind of lapse occurs just in your head. Perhaps a child is sitting next to you on the couch or climbing on you. You begin to daydream (fantasize) or get an uncomfortable feeling about touching the child's private parts. If you don't stop the fantasy, this is also called a lapse, because it places you that much closer to the forbidden sexual act. It makes it much harder to turn away. (Lapses are not bad acts in themselves, but are danger signals you need to do something about.)

Giving Up is where you figure you have already crossed the line, you have failed, and there is no turning back, so you may as well commit the sex offense. You're at the dangerous "Oh, what the hell! I may as well do it" point. When you get very close to reoffending, after a lapse like one of the two examples above, it is very easy to slip into the *Giving Up* stage.

This may be clearer to you if you think about some other *Giving Up* circumstance in your life. For example, maybe your mother has cooked a batch of fudge to give away as Christmas presents. You decide to sneak a piece. You tell yourself, "She'll never know." It tastes so good, you decide to take just one more. Then another. At this point you reach the *Giving Up* stage. It's the point where you feel there is no turning back. Obviously, she will notice some of the fudge has disappeared and will punish you, so you may as well eat the whole pan. In the case of sex offending, you tell yourself that you have gone too far to stop and give up trying.

Offense is molesting a child or raping someone.

Another way of looking at an offense chain is like a pit. In the bottom center is gooey mud (the offense) which you want to avoid. You get closer and closer to the muddy bottom as you fall deeper and deeper in from the sides (move from step to step, from the SUD inward to the Offense).

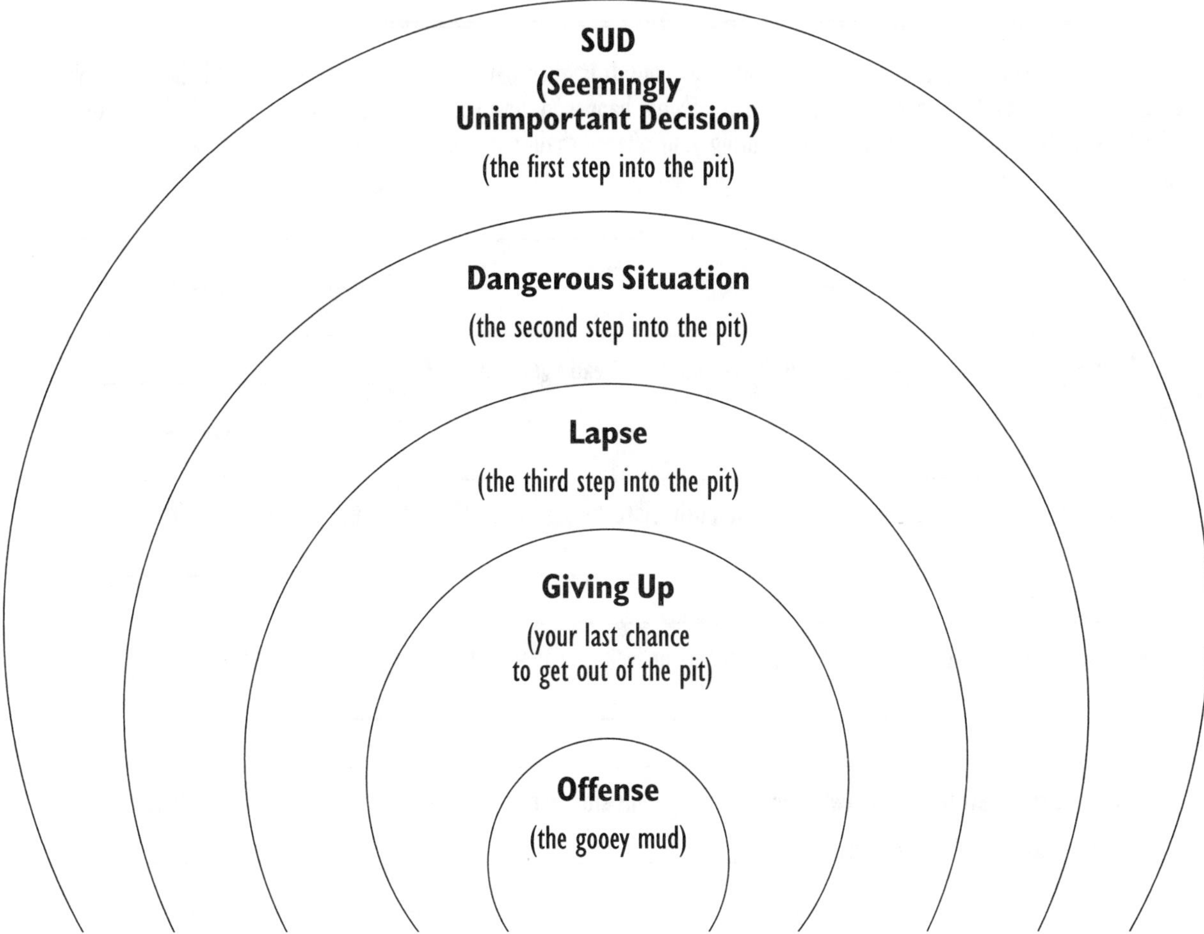

Let's look at what Bill could have done instead of committing the offense, how he could have changed his behavior at each step of the chain.

SUD stage: Bill could have said no to the neighbor: "I'm sorry, I can't watch your child, but I'll make some phone calls to find someone who can." But if he failed to do that and progressed to the *Dangerous Situation* stage, it wasn't too late. He still had options to get himself out of the situation.

Dangerous Situation stage: Bill could have called his parents, another neighbor or a friend and asked them to watch the child instead. But if he didn't do that and proceeded to the *Lapse* stage, he still could have avoided reoffending.

Lapse stage: At this point he could have immediately gotten up and left the room or premises, asked someone else to help, or even called the police to come get the child, if necessary. He could look at his reminder card for help with the coping strategies he learned in treatment. But if he failed again, he has one last chance at the *Giving Up* stage.

Giving Up stage: It is still not too late for Bill to stop. His best bet is to just get out of there, once he has made sure the child is safe. Touching the child's leg is not as serious as touching the child's private areas or molesting the child in some other way. If Bill got out of the house, he would never get to the *Offense* stage.

EXERCISE 1. OFFENSE CHAIN

Now it is time for you to make your own offense chain. It is often hard to remember exactly what happened. If you have problems, just think back to your offense first. Think of what happened, how you felt, and what you did right before that all the way back as far back as you can remember. Figuring your offense chain out backwards usually makes it easier. Just write what happened step by step.

Offense: (what you did)____

____

____

Giving Up: (at what point did you figure you had already gone too far?)________________

____

____

Lapse: (what did you do that was dangerously close to the act and/or when and how did you first fantasize about or get close to doing it?) Act(s): ________________________________

____

Fantasies (daydreams about doing the sexual act) or feelings connected to doing the sexual act:__________

____

____

Dangerous Situation: (what was the dangerous situation or dynamic you were in that came before or led to the fantasies, feelings, or acts?)____________________________________

____

____

____

SUD (Seemingly Unimportant Decision): (what happened and what decisions did you make that seemed reasonable at the time, but put you in that position of danger?) ____________________

____

____

____

____

When you finish this exercise, look closely at it. Read each step, beginning with the SUD first, back through to your offense. Can you see how that very first choice made the offense possible? Did you notice that you could have gotten out of the dangerous situation immediately? And what could you have done when you either started fantasizing, had a feeling, or did some act that was very close to offending? Was it really too late to stop after that, or could you have avoided taking that final step and committing the sex offense?

These are the questions you will be exploring in a variety of ways as you move through this workbook. But first, let's see how you can change your own offense scenario.

EXERCISE 2. ALTERNATIVE BEHAVIOR CHAIN

Fill in what you could have done instead at each step of the *Offense Chain* that would have kept you from offending. We will call this the *Alternative Behavior Chain*. The alternatives are what you have to remember in the future.

SUD Alternative:____

____

____

Dangerous Situation Alternative: ____________________________

____

____

Lapse Alternative: ____

____

____

Giving Up Alternative: _____________________________________

____

____

Result: No Offense.

Now reread what you wrote. You will notice that your alternative behaviors fall into either of two important categories: *Avoidance* or *Escape*. If you can *avoid* getting into a dangerous situation in the first place, you have the best chance of not offending because the opportunity is not present. But even if you get into a place of danger, lapse, or are ready to give up, you can still break the chain and not reoffend by *escaping* from the situation. Leaving is usually the most foolproof way of preventing reoffense. But there are also other ways. If your offense is child molestation, you should avoid being alone in the same room with a child, make sure others are there with you when a child is present, or if trapped in a situation where only you and a child are present, stay in another room or beyond arm's distance from any child.

Avoidance and *Escape* are the two most important words you will ever learn. Inscribe them permanently in your brain. Think of them every time you have to make a decision about where to go or what to do. Remember, if you can *avoid* being in a dangerous place, it is easiest not to offend. And if you find yourself at risk, *escape*. Get out of there fast. Get some protection for yourself.

I know you are saying to yourself, "That's silly. I don't have any desire to offend now. Why should I have to change my behavior by always having to avoid and escape?" Again, think of it as an insurance policy. If you are not in a situation of danger or leave a dangerous situation immediately, you are less likely to slip. Protect yourself by using these two simple words to think ahead and keep yourself safe: *avoid* and *escape*.

EXERCISE 3. AVOIDANCE AND ESCAPE

This is an exercise to help you remember *Avoidance* and *Escape*. First, take the word *Avoidance* and think of as many words or phrases as you can that have the same meaning. Then take the word *Escape* and do the same. For example, another phrase for *Avoidance* may be "staying away from," and another word for *Escape* is "getting away." Feel free to ask your friends and family for help.

Avoidance can also be thought of as: ______ ______________________________

______________________________ ______________________________

______________________________ ______________________________

______________________________ ______________________________

______________________________ ______________________________

______________________________ ______________________________

______________________________ ______________________________

______________________________ ______________________________

Escape can also be thought of as: ________ ______________________________

______________________________ ______________________________

______________________________ ______________________________

______________________________ ______________________________

______________________________ ______________________________

______________________________ ______________________________

______________________________ ______________________________

______________________________ ______________________________

If you can't think of any other words or phrases which mean the same as *Avoidance* and *Escape,* go to your dictionary. Look up these words. The dictionary will give you some words and phrases you can use to complete this exercise, and might help you better understand what these words mean.

Remember to use *Escape* and *Avoidance* properly, however. Use them only to keep from getting into dangerous situations or trouble. Avoiding talking about your offense, avoiding therapy, avoiding feelings, or avoiding people in general will only help you get into more trouble in the future. Likewise, if you escape from your responsibilities or from dealing with your problems, you will only make things more difficult for yourself in the long run. Don't just apply these concepts or any others blindly. Use reason and common sense.

Just to make sure you understand when and when not to *Escape* or *Avoid,* complete the following short exercise.

EXERCISE 4. USING AVOIDANCE AND ESCAPE PROPERLY

Write "yes" in front of each example where *Avoidance* or *Escape* is used properly and "no" before each example where it is misused.

1) ___________________ John previously molested his 5-year-old sister. He is working in a grocery store. A little girl tells him she needs to use the bathroom, and asks him to take her to it. John *avoids* being alone with the child by asking another clerk to show her to the bathroom.

2) ___________________ Doreen previously molested a 5-year-old neighbor boy while babysitting. On the way back from school one afternoon, she cut through a deserted park. She decided to swing on one of the swings. A little boy she knew came up and sat in the swing next to her and asked to be pushed. Doreen said "no" and left, *escaping* the situation.

3) ___________________ Albert was frustrated with some situations that happened at school, and found that he was thinking about exposing himself. When asked in group how he was doing, he said fine, *avoiding* thinking or talking about his exposure fantasies.

4) ___________________ Robert's father yelled at him, because he hadn't taken the garbage out. Robert ran away to *escape* from his father's anger.

5) ___________________ Carlos was with friends who wanted to have sex with a 16-year-old girl they considered a "slut." They talked about taking her into their garage and paying her to have sex with all of them. Carlos said "count me out" and left, *escaping* from the situation.

6) ___________________ Tony had previously molested a young boy. His sister was babysitting a young child. His sister had an emergency and had to leave, dumping the child on Tony. Tony walked out, *escaping*, leaving the child all alone, and called someone else to watch the child..

7) ___________________ Bill found himself peeking into the girls' washroom at school. He was very embarrassed about his behavior, but since he hadn't been caught he didn't tell anyone, thus *avoiding* further embarrassment or consequences.

8) ___________________ Maria was very unhappy. The last time she was unhappy, she had molested her foster sister. Maria decided to go to her own room, where nobody would see her unhappiness and bother her about it. (Was this *avoidance* or *escape*? Circle which one you think it is, then write yes or no in the blank.)

9) ___________________ Kamal refused to talk about his offense, saying he had put it behind him. (Was this *avoidance* or *escape*? Circle one.)

10) ___________________ Aaron was at a party. Everyone was getting loaded. There was a 14-year-old girl who had passed out on the bed in the bedroom. As Aaron was picking up his coat from the bed, he accidentally brushed her breast with his arm. It excited him. He ran out of the room. (Was this *avoidance* or *escape*? Circle one.)

If you are not sure about the answers to any of these, talk to your counselor or the other kids in group. These questions should help you remember when *Avoidance* and *Escape* are properly and improperly used.

For a final exercise on this subject, please fill in what would have been an appropriate *avoidance* or *escape* maneuver to prevent the risk of reoffense.

EXERCISE 5. USING ALTERNATIVE BEHAVIORS

Complete the following scenarios by writing in an appropriate alternative *escape* or *avoidance* behavior that could break the offense chain.

1) Juan previously molested a child. One afternoon, when he is alone in the garage fixing his bike, a neighbor child comes into the garage and starts to talk to him. Juan should____________________

2) Mark has exposed his penis to people before. A young woman comes to the door selling magazines. Mark invites her in. He fantasizes exposing himself in front of her. He unbuttons his pants and begins to pull down his zipper. He should_____

3) Jane is babysitting. She is changing a baby's diaper, when she has the urge to put her fingers in the little girl's vagina. She should ____________________

4) Ron and his girlfriend begin to make love. He is about to enter her when she says stop and tries to pull away from him. He should ____________________

5) In the last scenario, Ron doesn't want to stop, and he believes his girlfriend doesn't want to either. He decides to continue despite her protests. She begins to cry. He should____________________

6) Philip has previously exposed himself to young children on a school playground. He is working as a deliveryman for a florist. He notices that the most direct route to his next delivery is right past a school. He is late. He should ____________

7) Dan has previously molested two little boys. He is over at Tim's house, playing Nintendo in Tim's room, when Tim's mother tells Tim he must come downstairs and take the garbage out. Tim's younger brother shares the room and is due home any minute. Dan should ____________________

8) In the same scenario, Dan decides to finish his game. Tim's younger brother comes in the room before Dan finishes. Dan should ____________________

____

____

____

9) Next, Tim's younger brother asks Dan to help him with his homework. Dan sits on the brother's bed, next to him, and starts to help him. Dan begins to fantasize touching the brother's private parts. Dan should ____________________

____

____

____

10) Then, Dan places his hand on Tim's brother's leg. He begins to feel like a failure, because he has forgotten all the Relapse Prevention lessons he had learned in his treatment group. He figures Tim's brother will tell that he put his hand on the brother's leg, so, what the hell, why not touch his penis? At this point, Tim should ____________________

____

____

____

____

11) John is in a treatment program for sex offenders. His roommate says, "Hey, John. I've got an awful stiff neck. Would you rub it for me?" Both boys know that physical contact is against the rules. John begins to massage his roommate's neck and feels himself getting aroused. John should ____________________

____

____

____

Think of some situations in your own life where, if you don't use the appropriate *avoidance* and *escape* actions, you could be in a dangerous situation, lapse, give up, or reoffend. What *avoidance* and *escape* actions could you have taken at each step? Discuss this with your group or your therapist.

SUMMARY

What could you have learned from this chapter? You now know:

1) What **Relapse Prevention** means

2) The steps in an Offense Chain *(SUD, Dangerous Situation, Lapse, Giving Up, Offense)*

3) The steps in your own behavioral chain

4) Alternative actions you could have taken to prevent offending

5) The importance and use of *Avoidance* and *Escape* to prevent reoffense or accusations

If you feel confused about any of these ideas, read the chapter over, talk to your treatment provider, or talk to your friends in group.

NOTES

CHAPTER TWO

CHANGING THOUGHTS

Whether you move down the Offense Chain to reoffense or successfully avoid or escape offending is very much related to your thoughts. The way you think about things determines the way you feel about them, and the way you feel determines how you are likely to behave. For example, imagine that you are walking down the stairs at school. You feel a push on your shoulder from behind you. If you think that it is someone attacking you deliberately, you will probably feel angry, and you are likely to get back at the person in an aggressive way. But if you think that the person who pushed you did it by accident and didn't mean to, you probably won't feel bothered by it, and you won't take any action.

Another example: your father comes home and yells at you for not cleaning up the kitchen right. If you think to yourself, "I can't do anything right," you will feel bummed out possibly for the rest of the day, and probably either retreat to your room to mope or get angry at someone else. If, however, you say to yourself, "Dad must have had a tough day at work today. It's not me he's mad at. It must be someone or something at work," you won't feel as bad or take it as personally. Then you will probably stay out of your father's way until his mood improves, and go on with your usual activities.

A sexual abuse example: you have stayed late at school and hardly anyone is around. You think to yourself, "It can't hurt to just daydream about exposing my penis to a girl. Nobody would get hurt." You allow yourself to fantasize and feel sexually excited. If you then see a girl all alone in the hall, you are much more likely to expose yourself. On the other hand, if you say to yourself, "I need to think of something safer for me; fantasizing could get me in trouble again," and change your thoughts to plans for the basketball game coming up, you are less likely to get in trouble. You won't be sexually aroused and may not even notice the girl in the hall.

Thoughts are not engraved in stone. People change their ideas as they gain new information or views on an issue. When children are very little, they often have wild ideas about the way things work. For example, a young child may believe that there is a little person in the traffic light box who changes the color of the lights, or the child may believe a Tooth Fairy leaves money under her pillow in exchange for her baby teeth. As the child gains information about the world, he or she learns that the lights are controlled by electricity and that the "Tooth Fairy" is really Mom or Dad.

You too can change your thoughts, not just automatically when you gain new knowledge, but deliberately. You can tell yourself that your thinking is harmful, and change the way you see or think about a particular incident. For instance, in the very first example, where you are pushed, you might initially think that the push was deliberate. But you can tell yourself, "That's silly. Nobody has any reason to push me. It must have been an accident."

Self-talk is all the things people say to themselves to interpret the world, what is happening around them, and why they think it is happening. Self-talk can be negative or positive. You can change negative self-talk (that leads you closer to offending behavior, even by just making you feel bad about yourself) into positive self-talk (that makes you less likely to offend by reinforcing your competence and ability to control your own behavior) by changing your thoughts. When your self-talk is more positive, like saying to yourself, "It must have been an accident," your mood will usually change with it. You will probably go from feeling angry to not being bothered or concerned, and you will be less likely to act out your first angry feelings.

Sometimes people act *before* they think or feel or before they are *aware* of their feelings or thoughts. If you are one of these impulsive people, you need to slow your reactions down. Tell yourself that you won't react to anything until you have had time to think it over. Ahead of time, think about ways to slow down, like taking five deep breaths before you respond to anything, or reading over a card you carry with you reminding you to slow down.

In the following exercise, see how you can change your thinking from thoughts that would make you mad or sad to self-talk that will change your mood. What would you tell yourself instead?

EXERCISE 6. CHANGING SELF-TALK

1) Barry's brother tells him he is stupid. At first, Barry believes him and feels worthless. What can Barry tell himself to feel better?

____

____

____

2) Mario likes a girl in his class. He goes up to her and asks her if she'd like to go to the dance with him. She says she is busy. At first he doesn't believe her and thinks to himself that she must think he is a real nerd. He feels totally bummed out. How can Mario change his self-talk so that he will feel better? ______________________________

____

____

____

3) Danny does the best job he can on a school project, but the teacher gives him a "D." Danny thinks, "I must be stupid," and feels depressed. What could he say to himself that would make him feel better? ______________________________

____

____

____

4) Gloria auditions for jazz choir. The teacher doesn't pick her. She thinks to herself, "I must not be able to sing." Since singing has been her career goal, she feels destroyed. What could she tell herself that would make her feel better? __________

____

____

____

5) Several of the guys Joe likes make fun of him in class. Joe thinks they must not like him, and he feels sad. What could he say to himself that might make him feel better? ______________________________

____

____

____

6) Rick is ordered to participate in group therapy as a condition of probation. He thinks, "Only crazy people go to psychologists. I'm not crazy, so I won't go." He doesn't go, and gets put in Juvenile Hall. What should he have told himself instead that might have prevented this outcome? ______________________

____

____

7) Franco gets nervous and can't seem to get any words out when a girl he likes talks to him. He thinks, "I'm hopeless. I'll never have a girlfriend." He feels awful. What could he say to himself that would make him feel better? __________

____

____

____

8) Joey's father criticizes everything he does. Joey thinks it is hopeless to try to please his father, so he stops trying. How could Joey change his self-talk so that he would feel better and not give up? ______________________

____

____

____

9) Lisa is bummed out because she thinks the only reason her boyfriend likes her is for sex. What can she say to herself that can make her feel better about herself and not feel obligated to have sex with him? ______________________

____

____

____

10) Some bullies at school steal Julio's lunch and threaten to beat him up. Julio feels powerless. He thinks the only way he can be powerful is to join a gang. How can he change his thinking so that he feels stronger without having to join a gang?

____

____

____

11) Ruth is in a residential program for sex offenders. She is sure that everyone thinks she's a pervert. What can she say to herself so she can feel better? ______________________

____

____

Every time we do something, it is usually triggered by some event that starts a kind of chain reaction. Included in this chain reaction are thoughts, self-talk, feelings, and finally, actions. For example, if a teacher gives you a hard time, you say to yourself, "She's picking on me. It's not fair. She lets other kids get away with worse." This self-talk makes you feel angry and resentful. If you feel angry, you are more likely to yell at or punch some other person who gets in your way.

In the next exercise, pick a situation where everything turned out horribly, where you said or did something you were sorry about later. First, trace back your self-talk, your feelings, and the behaviors that resulted, and write them on the left side of the page. Then go back and change your negative thoughts, and determine what your feelings and actions could have been as a result on the right hand side of the page.

EXERCISE 7. CHANGING NEGATIVE THOUGHTS

1) Think of a time in your life where you got mad or upset and said or did something you wish you hadn't. What happened that started the chain? (What triggered the unhappy result?) ____________________

____

2) What did you say to yourself? (What thoughts did you have?) ____________________

____

____

3) How did you feel? ____

____

____

4) What did you do (that turned out badly)? ______________________________

____

5) What could you have said to yourself instead? ____________________________

____

6) How do you think you would have felt if you had changed your thoughts to those above instead? __________

____

7) What do you think you would have done instead if you felt differently? ____________________

____

In the last chapter, we talked about *Offense Chains*. At each step of the *offense chain,* the offender chose behaviors that brought him or her closer and closer to the offending act. By choosing and using *avoidance* and *escape* techniques instead, an offender could prevent him- or herself from reoffending. You learned that the earlier in the chain the person avoided or escaped, the less likely he or she would commit the offense. Remember that it is never too late to change behaviors until the offense has been committed.

Self-talk plays a part in the offense chain and in changing behaviors. Depending on what you say to yourself, you are more or less likely to move down the offense chain or deeper into the pit. For example, if a boy who molested a young child says to himself, "I can be alone with children. I'll never molest again," he is more likely to place himself in a dangerous situation than someone who says to himself, "I don't want to take any risks. I don't even want anyone to *think* I might be sexually interested in a child."

Now let's look at how self-talk affected the scenario we discussed in the first chapter. Before choosing to babysit for the desperate mother, Bill probably said to himself, "This poor mother needs me. I can't say 'no.' It couldn't hurt to help her." On the surface, this sounds like a *Seemingly Unimportant Decision.*

Once in the *Dangerous Situation* – being alone with the child – Bill probably said to himself, "I'm not in any danger. I won't do anything wrong. The mother will be back soon, anyhow."

When he reached the *Lapse* stage, he told himself, "It's okay to fantasize about a sexual activity with this child as long as I don't do anything," or, "Touching this child, even accidentally, sure felt nice."

Then, he probably *Gave Up*, saying to himself, "I'm a failure already. I may as well go ahead with the offense," or, "I'll just touch him one time. No one will ever know." And then came the full *Offense*.

Instead, if Bill had changed his self-talk to self-protective escape and avoidance types of statements, he probably would not have offended. In the next exercise write what Bill's alternative self-talk could have been: what he could have thought or said to himself that would have kept him from moving down the offense chain.

EXERCISE 8. ALTERNATIVE THOUGHTS DOWN THE OFFENSE CHAIN

Based on Bill's story in Chapter One, fill in the blanks with self-talk which, if he acted accordingly, would have stopped him from committing the sex offense.

SUD (when the mother asked him to babysit): ______________________________

____

____

Dangerous Situation (once he was alone with the child): ______________________________

____

____

Lapse (when he fantasized touching the child): ______________________________

____

____

(when he touched the child's leg): ______________________________

____

____

Giving Up (when he felt lost, like it was too late to quit): ______________________________

____

____

Now look back at your own offense chain. You probably said things to yourself or felt things that were a lot like the thoughts and feelings in Bill's scenario, even though you may not have been consciously aware at the time of what you were thinking and feeling. In the next exercise, you will reconstruct your original thoughts and feelings, then write what you should have thought or said to yourself instead. The purpose of this is to make certain that if you are ever in similar circumstances again, you won't go down that same chain toward offending. Your new, improved model of thinking will prevent it. Had you been able to change your thinking prior to your offense, the whole course of your history might have been different.

EXERCISE 9. CHANGING YOUR OWN THOUGHTS (SELF-TALK)

At each step of your own *Offense Chain*, write down what probably went through your mind to put you in the situation, then write what you could have thought and said to yourself instead which would have kept you from moving down the chain.

Seemingly Unimportant Decision (SUD): The choice you made: ______________________

____

What you probably thought or felt at the time: ______________________

____

What you could have changed your thoughts to instead: ______________________

____

____

Dangerous Situation: The dangerous situation you got yourself into: ______________________

____

What you probably thought or felt at the time: ______________________

____

What you could have changed your thoughts to instead: ______________________

____

____

Lapse: What you probably thought or felt at the time: ______________________

____

What you could have changed your thoughts to instead: ______________________

____

____

Giving Up: What you probably thought or felt at the time: ______________________

____

What you should have changed your thoughts to instead: ______________________

____

____

____

Now let's put the whole chain together with what you must have thought or felt and did and what alternative thoughts and behaviors would have kept you out of trouble at each step of the chain. You can do this chain either with the offense that got you here, or with some other offense or bad behavior you have committed in the past. Ask your group leader which would be the best way for you to do this exercise and/or try it each way.

EXERCISE 10. BEHAVIOR AND THOUGHT CHAIN AS IT WAS AND MODIFIED

On the solid lines below, write the negative steps you took both in acts and self-talk. On the dash lines write the good alternative behaviors and thoughts you might have said and done that would have kept you out of trouble. (If you don't understand this exercise, or have difficulty with it, ask your therapist or counselor for help. It is a hard one!)

THOUGHTS (SELF TALK) **BEHAVIORS**

SUD STAGE:

Alternatives

DANGEROUS SITUATION:

Alternatives

LAPSE:

Alternatives

GIVING UP:

Alternatives

OFFENSE:

NO OFFENSE:

Read your finished exercise over carefully. Really think about each step and how you could have behaved differently and thought differently so that you wouldn't have committed the offense. Apply this changed thinking and behavior to situations that could happen to you in the future. An offense-free life requires thinking before you act, and figuring out possible results of your actions and thoughts in advance.

SUMMARY

These are the major things you had the opportunity to learn from this chapter:

1) The relationship between thoughts or feelings and behavior
2) How you can change your thoughts (self-talk) for a more positive outcome
3) How to change negative thoughts down the *Offense Chain* to prevent offending
4) How thoughts and behavior fit together in the *Offense Chain*
5) The importance of thinking ahead to possible consequences

NOTES

CHAPTER THREE

STINKING THINKING

In this chapter we are going to look a little further at how negative, wrong, or distorted thinking, sometimes called "stinking thinking," can cause problems that may lead you down into the reoffense pit. You will learn different ways people use *stinking thinking*, what it can do, and how to change it so that you can step out of the Offense Chain. There are three types of stinking thinking we will discuss: *roadblocks*, *thinking distortions*, and *thinking errors*.

Roadblocks are obstacles you set up for yourself. When you use the words and phrases we will be looking at below, you are setting up roadblocks that prevent you from making positive changes. When you use these negative self-talk roadblocks, you will get stuck. For example, if you say, "I can't," you are deciding not to change or do things you may want to do. "I can't" usually means "I won't."

The same principles of changing thoughts or self-talk that you learned about in the last chapter can be applied to how you see your life and how you can make the changes you need to make. If you talk to yourself (and express yourself to others, too) in a positive way, you open all kinds of doors to new and better experiences.

Read over the following examples of negative and positive self-talk. See how the negative self-talk limits your options, while the positive alternatives give you power to change things. Then complete the "Eliminating Roadblocks" exercise that follows.

NEGATIVE SELF-TALK	POSITIVE SELF-TALK ALTERNATIVES
"I can't"	"I can't means I won't, but even though it may be difficult, I'll find a way if I want to badly enough."
"I have to"	"I want to" or "I choose to."
"I should"	"I may if I want to."
"I should have"	"I made a mistake, but it's not the end of the world. I can learn from it so I won't make the same mistake again."
"Yeah, but"	"I'll think about it."
"I don't have a choice"	"I do have a choice. I just have to look at the costs and benefits of my choices."
"You're stopping me from . . ."	"The only one stopping me from doing what I want or need to do is myself. And if there are reasons why I can't do something, I've either got to find some other ways of going about it, or make some other choices."

It is important to recognize that none of these statements is absolute. Sometimes a person is physically unable do something (like asking someone with a broken leg to play football) or is stopped from it or doesn't have a choice. But all too often we overuse these negative thoughts to hinder our progress. When you switch positive thoughts for your negative ones, you will feel more capable and actually will accomplish more. In addition, you will feel better about yourself and your life.

EXERCISE 11. ELIMINATING ROADBLOCKS

List three negative statements you have made (using the ones listed above or others) and the situations in which you made them. Then substitute three positive statements you could have made instead.

Negative statement and situation	Positive alternative statement
1) ______________________	1a) ______________________
______________________	______________________
______________________	______________________
2) ______________________	2a) ______________________
______________________	______________________
______________________	______________________
3) ______________________	3a) ______________________
______________________	______________________
______________________	______________________

There are other ways that our thinking may be twisted and can interfere with choosing a positive lifestyle. We call these **Thinking Distortions**. Some of the most common *Thinking Distortions* are:

1) **All or Nothing Thinking**: This is where you see everything as all good or all bad. It is often called "seeing things in black or white." Nothing in life is perfectly good or perfectly evil. Everything is a shade of gray. While you try to be the best person you can, you will never be perfect. If you expect absolute perfection of yourself, you will always be disappointed or consider yourself a failure. On the other hand, even if you do something awful, that doesn't make you a terrible person. You can learn from your mistakes and be an even better person in the future.

2) **Jumping to Conclusions**: In this kind of stinking thinking, you assume a negative result even though it hasn't yet happened and may not. This is called a negative expectation. You decide before all the evidence is in. An example is when you assume someone is thinking something bad about you , even though nothing like that was said! Another example is when you you expect things to go badly and don't allow for the possibility of a different outcome.

Perhaps someone is rude to you. You might jump to the conclusion that this person doesn't like you. It could be that the person is having a bad day or something else bad happened to that person that has nothing to do with you, and the person is so engrossed in bad feelings that he or she doesn't even think about you or being nice to you.

An example of *negative expectation* is where you expect that you won't have any fun at a school dance because your friends aren't going, so you don't go. You may have had fun there without them. You don't know until you try.

3) **Overgeneralizing:** This is where you think that because something bad happens once, it will always happen. For example, if someone you like turns you down once for a date, you conclude that he or she doesn't like you, or, worse yet, that no one you're interested in dating will like you. It may just be that the person is busy, or is involved with someone else. Maybe others will want to go on a date with you even if this person doesn't.

4) **Overemphasizing One Detail**: This is similar to *Overgeneralizing,* picking out one negative happening. In this case, however, you dwell on the one bad detail and ignore all the other good aspects. For example, if someone you like makes a joke about your nose, you consider your total looks a disaster, ignoring the fact that your friend likes your personality, compliments the way you dress, and thinks you're smart.

5) **Rejecting the Positive**: This is where you disqualify any positive features or happenings, insisting they don't count, so you can hold on to your negative beliefs. For example, someone tells you how nice your haircut is. You reject this positive statement, instead thinking to yourself that you are really a mess. The nice haircut doesn't count.

6) **Catastrophizing**: Similar to *Overemphasizing One Detail*, this is where you assume that *everything* bad is going to happen because one thing goes bad. For example, if you get a bad grade on one test, you assume you won't be able to pass the class and you'll flunk out of school and never get a job. Then you don't try. In reality, it may have been that the first test was a particularly hard one.

7) **Personalizing**: In this kind of *stinking thinking*, you blame yourself for things you have no control over, or assume there is something wrong with you if you receive negative treatment of some kind. For example, a bully might come up to you and call you a wimp or a bitch. You assume you must be a wimp or a bitch, rather than recognizing that the bully might have problems of his or her own and needs to call people negative names to build himself or herself up. Or, your parents may be fighting, and you assume it must be because you have misbehaved. In reality, they may be having marital problems that have nothing to do with what you did. They may be arguing about you as a way of taking out their anger toward each other.

8) **Calling Yourself Names:** In this type of *Thinking Distortion*, you attach a negative label to yourself rather than describe a negative behavior, error, or happening. For example, you might call yourself a "dumbbell" because you don't understand what is being taught in math, rather than just describing yourself as having some problems with the work. Or you might call yourself a "pervert," because you did a sexual offense you were ashamed of, rather than recognizing you committed a bad, hurtful act but most of the time are a good person. Can you see how labeling yourself can get in the way of doing something positive about an area where you have problems?

(You should be careful, however, not to deny or minimize the harm you did to your victim just because you are basically a good person. Good people acknowledge their wrongs and use their best efforts not to repeat them.)

There are special kinds of distorted thinking common to most sex offenders. These include: *misinterpreting what their victim is thinking*, such as believing the person is asking for sex when the person really isn't and doesn't want it; *excusing their sexual offenses,* such as telling themselves and others, "My father molested me, so it is okay for me to molest my sister"; *minimizing the harm they've done,* thinking, "It didn't bother me when it happened to me, so it won't bother my victim," or "He'll get over it. It was no big thing"; or *denying responsibility,* including saying, "He came to me; I didn't start it," or "I only did it because everyone else did. They started it. I didn't have any choice."

You can correct your **Thinking Distortions** just as you changed your self-talk in the *Roadblocks* above. In the next exercise, you will have the opportunity to correct your *Thinking Distortions* in a variety of situations. Have you ever committed any of these *Thinking Distortions* yourself? If you answered no, look again. We all fall into these traps sometimes.

EXERCISE 12. CORRECTING THINKING DISTORTIONS

For each of the following examples of *Thinking Distortions*, write what the person could have said to him/herself instead that would have been more positive.

1) **All or Nothing Thinking**: Richie and Chris have been going together. Chris is bright and well-liked, but Richie finds out that Chris had a bad reputation at a prior school. Even though he really likes Chris, he thinks, "I'm going to dump Chris, because Chris isn't the perfect person I thought." What would be a better way for Richie to think about this? ________

____

____

2) **Jumping to Conclusions:** Richie stays with Chris. One day he sees Chris in the hall with an arm around another person. He immediately assumes Chris has been lying to him about their relationship. What could he say to himself instead that might help him deal with this problem? ______________________________

____

____

3) **Overgeneralizing:** Terry tried out for the basketball team and didn't make it. Terry thought, "I'm no good at sports." What could Terry have said instead? ______________________________

____

____

4) **Overemphasizing One Detail:** Gloria is a warm, friendly person with dark, wavy hair and beautiful brown eyes. Gloria's father teased her about being fat. Because of that, she says to herself, "I'm ugly." What could Gloria have told herself instead? ______________________________

____

____

5) **Rejecting the Positive:** Jimmy feels very ugly because he is 30 pounds overweight. His friend tells him that he is good-looking and attractive. He says to himself, "So what? People think I'm ugly because I'm fat." How could he change his self-talk? What could he say instead? ______________________________

____

____

6) **Catastrophizing:** Rico loses his job. He thinks, "I'll never get a job again." What could he say to himself instead?

____

____

____

7) **Personalizing:** When Rico's boss told him he was fired, Rico thought, "He thinks I'm no good." What are some other things Rico could have said to himself that would have been less self-destructive? ______________________________

____

____

____

8) **Calling Yourself Names:** After Rico lost his job, he said to himself, "I'm a loser." ______________

____

____

What could he have said instead? ______________________________

____

Can you see how much better you will feel about yourself and/or how much better you will do if you reframe your thinking and don't fall into *Thinking Distortion* traps?

Thoughts are very complicated. We have seen how our thoughts affect our feelings and our behavior, and how we have the power to change them so that we feel better or behave in a more positive way.

How we take in information from around us is also a part of our thinking. We all perceive (take in) experiences differently, depending on what experiences we have had in the past. Since everyone has had different experiences, everyone perceives things differently. Sometimes we *think* we know what another person is thinking or feeling when we really don't. We only know what *we* might think, feel, or need in that situation. Often we make up okay-sounding reasons for behavior we know is wrong. This is called *rationalizing*. Rationalizing is one kind of *Thinking Error. Thinking Errors* and *cognitive distortions* mean the same thing.

When you committed your sexual offense, you made various types of *Thinking Errors*. You probably twisted around your thinking to make your negative behavior seem okay. For example, you may have touched a young child's private parts while wrestling. The child may not have said anything, so you thought to yourself, "She probably likes it and wants more," or "This won't hurt him," and you deliberately touched the child a second time. Or, you got a brief glimpse of an adult undressing through the window of a nearby house and thought to yourself, "If I sneak into the yard, maybe I can see the person in the nude. No one will notice me, because it's pretty dark out now. Since nobody will see me, I'm not doing anything wrong." These are *Thinking Errors*. Your thoughts weren't based on real facts. They led you into negative behaviors that invaded other people's privacy, and could result in reoffense and criminal charges.

How can you know if you are thinking correctly? One way is to stop and ask yourself some of following questions:

1) Is this something someone might find hurtful, embarrassing, or unpleasant?
2) Is this something I would feel uncomfortable telling my parents, teachers, counselors and friends about?
3) Is this something I wouldn't like someone to do to me if I were their age or in their situation?
4) Am I breaking any laws or rules by doing this?

5) Would there be negative consequences (would something bad happen to me) if I were caught doing this?

6) Would I feel kind of crummy about myself afterward if I did this?

If you answer "no" to all of the questions, your thinking is probably correct. If your answer is "yes" to *any* of them, however, you are probably engaging in thinking errors.

You can also check out your thinking by talking to parents, counselors, teachers and friends. Listen to what they have to say about the activity. If they all agree, and you do too, your thinking is probably correct. If they all agree, but you don't, your thinking is probably distorted. If one of the groups approves, but the rest don't, could that one group be wrong? Have these people gotten into trouble, or could they, for doing some of these things? If one of the groups disapproves, but all the others approve, could the disapproving group be out of line? They may have a different value system. Think about your own values. You probably know down underneath what is basically right and what is basically wrong.

We'll talk more about errors in judging what others are thinking, feeling, or experiencing in the chapter on Empathy later in this book. But the short exercise that follows will give you the opportunity to correct some common types of *Thinking Errors*. In the spaces, write what the true situation is more likely to be.

EXERCISE 13. CHANGING THINKING ERRORS

1) Albert goes into a neighbor's yard and peeps through a window to watch the neighbor dressing. He tells himself he isn't doing anything wrong and that he won't get caught. What would be more correct thinking? ____________________

____

____

____

2) Gloria tells herself she is just teaching her 10-year-old cousin about sex when she asks him to rub her breasts. What would be more correct thinking? ____________________

____

____

____

3) Kerry thinks it would be fun to "pants" (take down the pants of) a kindergartner at school. Kerry doesn't think this would do any harm. Correct Kerry's thinking. ____________________

____

____

____

4) Julio rubs up against girls on the bus. He thinks this is okay behavior because he thinks the girls like it. Correct his thinking.

____

____

____

____

5) Andy figures that if he threatens his little brother, his little brother won't tell anyone that Andy molested him. How should Andy change his thinking? ______________________________

____

____

____

6) Pat and a group of friends decide to rape someone as an initiation to a gang. Pat thinks, "This person is lucky to be chosen." Correct Pat's thinking. ______________________________

____

____

____

7) Dwayne exposes himself to a 6-year-old boy at school. He says to himself, "Nudity is good. Our society is too uptight. I'm really doing a good thing for this child." Correct his thinking error. ______________________________

____

____

____

8) Before she molests her little sister, Andrea says to herself, "My father did this to me, and he loved me, so why shouldn't I do the same thing to my little sister." Correct her thinking ______________________________

____

____

____

9) What was one of your thinking errors at the time you committed your offense? (If you don't remember any, just figure out what one must have been.) ______________________________

____

____

____

10) Correct your own thinking in question 9. ______________________________

____

____

____

So we all have some negative thoughts and need to change them. How can we do that? First, you need to recognize negative, wrong, or distorted thoughts, or, what we've called *stinking thinking.* The exercises you have already done in this workbook should help you be aware of them. Be sure you review this chapter every couple of weeks to remind yourself of the pitfalls.

If and when you fall into negative, wrong, or distorted thinking, however, there are a variety of techniques you can use to help you change your thinking. They include:

1) **Thought Stopping:** *Thought Stopping* is exactly what it says . . . just stopping the improper thoughts. But how can you do that? There are several ways:

A) Tell yourself to stop, or yell "stop" to yourself in your head or out loud, to throw the negative thoughts out of your mind.

B) Remind yourself of some of the awful consequences of your wrong thoughts if you act on them. For example, if you are thinking to yourself that your younger brother would probably enjoy having you touch his penis (which is a *Thinking Error),* you instead focus on what it will be like when the police come and take you away after he tells, or what it will be like when the police come to school to arrest you. You might also add to it the image of you escaping from the situation before you do anything wrong and feeling proud of yourself.

C) Use some type of outside stimuli to stop your thoughts, such as rubber bands or other measures advised by your therapist. Wearing a thick rubber band on your wrist and snapping it when you catch yourself in negative thinking, or carrying a jar of putrid smelling stuff (as recommended by your therapist) and taking a whiff can drive the negative thoughts away fast. (Talk to your therapist first, however, to determine whether any of these techniques are appropriate for you.)

2) **Thought Switching:** Once you have jarred yourself out of the negative thoughts, you have the power to change them to more appropriate ones. With the help of your therapist, you might even plan some *appropriate* fantasies or scenarios for yourself in advance. Write them down on a card and read them to yourself.

Another form of *Thought Switching* is to think of something entirely different, for example, something totally unrelated to sex offending like a history assignment or a new play in basketball. Or switch to the terrible consequences of offending rather than the pleasurable part.

3) **Get Help:** If you are still having trouble with thoughts that are dangerous or depressing, talk to someone you trust. Tell a good friend or family member. Call your therapist. Discuss the situation. Talking things out always helps.

4) **Record What You Are Thinking:** Often the people you can talk to about these issues aren't around when you need them, so keep pen and paper or a tape recorder handy and record what's going through your head. Then you can discuss what went through your mind later in therapy.

If you learn about any other techniques to change your thinking, write them here so you won't forget them: ____

____

____

SUMMARY

These are the major things you could have learned from this chapter:

1) Three types of *Stinking Thinking* that need to be changed

2) What your *Roadblocks* to productive activity and change are and how to correct them

3) Common *Thinking Distortions* and how to correct them

4) *Thinking Errors* relative to offenses and how to correct them

5) Techniques to help you *change* your thinking

CHAPTER FOUR

EMOTIONS

Just as what you are thinking affects how you feel and behave, your emotions (the way you feel) affect what you are thinking and what you do. When you are feeling depressed, ineffective, powerless, and angry, you are more likely to employ distorted or wrong thinking and to behave in a way that is destructive or dangerous to yourself or others.

Many people who have done sexual offenses are out of touch with what they are feeling. They have closed off their emotions because of childhood abuses and problems. They act out their feelings instead of allowing themselves to experience the feelings – like hitting someone instead of just feeling anger. If they cannot feel their own emotions, they certainly cannot feel what their victims might be experiencing. For these reasons, we will spend a lot of pages in this workbook on your emotions, emotional needs, and awareness of the feelings of others.

First, it is important to develop a vocabulary of feelings. The following is a list of some of the words we use to describe our emotions:

FEELING WORDS

afraid
aggravated
aloof
amused
angry
anxious
ashamed
bashful
bored
cautious
cheerful
cold
content
courageous
curious
defiant
depressed

detached
determined
dirty
disgusted
down
dumb
ecstatic
embarrassed
energetic
excited
exhausted
fearful
flippant
frantic
friendly
frightened
frustrated

good
goofy
grateful
guilty
happy
hateful
helpless
hopeful
hopeless
hostile
humiliated
hungry
hurt
hyper
hysterical
inadequate
impatient

independent
indifferent
insecure
irritated
isolated
jealous
joyful
lonely
loving
mad
nervous
optimistic
overwhelmed
panicked
paranoid
peppy
perplexed

pessimistic
playful
pleased
powerful
put-out
regretful
relieved
resentful
responsible
ridiculous
rotten
sad
satisfied
selfish
sexy
shaky
shy

silly
smothered
sorry
stupid
tearful
thankful
threatened
tough
troubled
unhappy
unique
uptight
vengeful
whipped
wicked
worried
wounded

Read over the feeling words listed. Think about what they mean. (If you don't know the meaning of a word, look it up in the dictionary). Can you think of a time in your life when you felt the way each word describes? In your treatment group, write the words on separate cards or pieces of paper. Play charades with them, acting them out for others to guess. Think of other feeling words that aren't on the list.

The following three exercises will increase your understanding and use of feeling words.

EXERCISE 14. USING FEELING WORDS

1) Write a short story or poem using 12 of the feeling words from the list above (use extra paper if you need it):

2) On separate sheets of blank paper draw a picture or design that expresses each of the following feeling words:

rage sorrow joy nervousness power weakness

EXERCISE 15. FEELINGS SENTENCE COMPLETION

1) Complete the following sentences, describing the situation when you have felt the feeling listed:

a) I felt great when ________________

b) I worry that ________________

c) I am most angry that ________________

d) I feel loneliest when ________________

e) I felt appreciated when ________________

f) I felt abandoned when ________________

g) I felt inadequate when ________________

h) I am calmest when ________________

i) I am frustrated with ________________

j) I felt excited when ________________

k) I feel bitter towards ________________

2) Now do the same type of exercise the other way around. This time describe the feeling *after* the situation. Complete the following sentences, using different feeling words for each.

a) When someone is *rude* to me, I feel ________________

b) When someone is *kind* to me, I feel ________________

c) If I were given a *surprise party*, I would feel ________________

d) When I say something *stupid*, I feel ________________

e) If someone held a *gun* to my head I would feel ________________

f) When all my friends are *out of town*, I feel ________________

g) When *I can't* do something I am *trying* to do, I feel ________________

h) Just before *test grades* are given out, I feel ________________

i) When I talk to someone I *really like*, I feel ________________

j) When I'm *criticized*, I feel ________________

k) When I *win* at a sport, I feel ________________

EXERCISE 16. RECORDING EMOTIONS

Record what you are feeling at the following times of the day for three days.

a) First thing in the morning when you are awakened:

Day #1____

Day #2____

Day #3____

b) During lunchtime:

Day #1____

Day #2____

Day #3____

c) Mid-afternoon before school is out:

Day #1____

Day #2____

Day #3____

d) Right after school:

Day #1____

Day #2____

Day #3____

e) Just before you go to bed:

Day #1____

Day #2____

Day #3____

The exercises above were designed to help you begin to think about your feelings and develop a vocabulary to express those emotions. Did you have difficulty with the last part? Or find yourself writing "Okay" or "the same" on each of the lines? While your emotions at these different times may not have been very different or extreme, there may have been events that triggered stronger emotions that you were not conscious of feeling.

One way of determining how you feel is to check in with your body. Your body will give you clues as to what emotion you are feeling, if you pay attention. For example, if you are angry:

1) Does your face get red or feel hot?

2) Do your muscles tense up?

3) Does your breathing change?

4) Do you feel sick?

5) Does your voice go up in pitch?

6) Does your head pound?

7) Do you feel more energetic or powerful?

8) Does your posture change? How?

You probably will experience some, but not all, of these physical signs of anger. Be aware of which ones apply to you. Then, for example, if you find your muscles tensing, voice going up, and energy pulsing, you can clue yourself in that you are probably feeling angry.

When you are depressed, you are likely to slump, cross your arms over your chest to keep people out, speak more softly or mumble, and/or frown. When you are anxious or nervous, you are likely to fidget and tap, move around a lot, feel racy inside, your voice may get quavery, and you may have difficulty sleeping. Every time your body language changes, check in on what emotions you may be feeling, and every time you are aware of your emotions, check in on how your body is reacting. Especially for people who tend to impulsively act out their emotions, this is a way of slowing down and taking more well-thought-out actions.

Although anger, frustration, and other painful emotions play a part in your sexual offending, there are no "bad" emotions. All feelings are normal and okay. It is what you *do* with the emotions that is important. If you are aware of your emotions and appropriately express them, you are less likely to reoffend.

How have you handled your emotions in the past? In the next exercise, you will look at the various ways you may have expressed several different emotions. Did your parents handle feelings in the same way? How did you feel when they handled their feelings toward you in that way?

EXERCISE 17. EXPRESSING EMOTIONS

1) **Anger:**

a) How many of the following ways have you expressed or handled your anger? Put a check mark next to the ones that apply.

_____ 1) Yelled or screamed

_____ 2) Hit someone

_____ 3) Hit something

_____ 4) Broke something

_____ 5) Cried

_____ 6) Ran away

_____ 7) Just held it in

_____ 8) Wrote out your feelings

_____ 9) Drank or used drugs

_____ 10) Gave the silent treatment

_____ 11) Said something nasty

_____ 12) Took out your feelings on someone other than who you were mad at

_____ 13) Said something to hurt someone back

_____ 14) Ran or did other physical exercise

_____ 15) Swore

_____ 16) Said something sarcastic

_____ 17) Did something creative (art, woodwork or?)

_____ 18) Had revenge

_____ 19) Took a time out

_____ 20) Talked out your feelings calmly at the time

_____ 21) Talked out your feelings calmly a little later

_____ 22) Committed a sex offense

_____ 23) Changed your thinking about the situation

_____ 24) Took out your feelings on yourself:
cut yourself _____
attempted suicide _____
other _____

Any other ways? ____

____

b) Which of these ways of expressing anger are most healthy or productive for you? Circle the numbers. Why do you think they are healthy or work best? ____

____

____

c) Look at your most unhealthy responses. Why are they unproductive ways of expressing anger? ______________

____

d) Based on what you have learned in the last chapter about how changing your thoughts can affect how you feel about things, what could you say to yourself that might make you feel less angry? ______________________

____

____

2) **Depression** (feeling down or blue): ____

____

____

a) How many of the following ways have you expressed or handled your depression? (Check the ones you've used.)

_____ 1) Cried
_____ 2) Read
_____ 3) Drank
_____ 4) Hurt yourself
_____ 5) Used drugs
_____ 6) Ate
_____ 7) Attempted suicide How? ______________
_____ 8) Got angry
_____ 9) Withdrew (stayed alone)
_____ 10) Wrote out your feelings
_____ 11) Ran or did other physical exercise
_____ 12) Did something creative
_____ 13) Hit something
_____ 14) Took your feelings out on someone else (including sex offending)
_____ 15) Watched TV
_____ 16) Slept
_____ 17) Had sex
_____ 18) Beat someone up
_____ 19) Talked to a friend
_____ 20) Moaned
_____ 21) Other ways? ______________

b) Circle the ways you expressed depression in a positive way. Why are these healthy? ______________

____

____

____

c) Now look at your most destructive (unhealthy) ways. Why are they harmful? ______________

____

____

____

d) What could you say to yourself to help you feel less depressed? ______________

____

____

3) **Anxiety** (worry, nervousness, etc.):

a) How many of the following ways have you expressed or handled your anxiety? (Check the ones you've used)

__ 1) Dwelled on it (kept worrying)
__ 2) Paced
__ 3) Yelled or screamed
__ 4) Cried
__ 5) Withdrew (stayed alone)
__ 6) Ran away
__ 7) Overate and threw up
__ 8) Held your feelings in
__ 9) Wrote out your feelings
__ 10) Did something creative
__ 11) Punched the wall
__ 12) Struck someone
__ 13) Made lists of things to do
__ 14) Ran/physical exercise
__ 15) Talked about your feelings with someone who would understand
__ 16) Took out your feelings on yourself (cut yourself, attempted suicide, other)

b) Again, circle the most positive or healthy ways of expressing anxiety. Then look at the unhealthy or destructive ways you have handled your anxiety. Can you see why they were not healthy for you? ________________________

____

____

c) Think of positive self-talk that might make you feel a little less anxious. What could you say to yourself? ________

____

____

You can do the same kind of exercise with any of your emotions that bother you or cause you problems, such as frustration, powerlessness, loneliness, hopelessness, resentment, jealousy, fear, or humiliation. There are lots of these painful emotions. Think of some you especially tend to feel, and write them down.

It is also important to look carefully at what *triggers* these painful emotions. Just as the trigger of a gun shoots it off, *emotional triggers* shoot you into a painful emotional state. *Emotional triggers* are events or happenings that "set you off." For example, a white person calling an African-American a "nigger" is a *trigger* for anger or rage. Most people's anger is triggered when they feel put down, used, betrayed, frustrated, not treated fairly, or disrespected.

Depression may be triggered by many of the same experiences as anger is, and it can also be triggered by experiences where people feel helpless, inadequate, worthless or like a failure, or when they are lonely.

Anxiety is often triggered by uncertainty, lack of control, and inability to solve a problem.

Sometimes we are not aware of the triggering event and don't realize what "set us off." We think we feel the way we do for some reason that has nothing to do with what really started our painful emotions. At other times events may build one upon the other, so there may be multiple triggers.

Think of some of the times you felt angry, depressed, and anxious. Can you identify the triggering events? If you can identify and understand your triggers and how you tend to react, you are more likely to be able to make choices about how to respond in less negative ways. You may be able to choose behaviors or say things to yourself (change your self-talk) that will help you feel better more quickly.

The next exercise helps you to understand the tie-in between your emotions, your triggers, what you say to yourself, and the outcomes or results, and how you can either make yourself feel better or worse, depending on how you *think* about what has happened.

EXERCISE 18: CHANGING EMOTIONS AND OUTCOMES

1) First, think of three times you felt really rotten – frustrated, angry, depressed, or whatever – and there were negative outcomes or results from the experiences. Write down the emotion you felt at the time, identify the triggering event (what happened that brought it on), what you thought and said to yourself at the time, and what the negative result was.

EMOTION	TRIGGERING EVENT	NEGATIVE SELF-TALK	RESULT
1) ________	________________	________________	________________
	________________	________________	________________
	________________	________________	________________
	________________	________________	________________
2) ________	________________	________________	________________
	________________	________________	________________
	________________	________________	________________
	________________	________________	________________
3) ________	________________	________________	________________
	________________	________________	________________
	________________	________________	________________
	________________	________________	________________

2) For the next part of this exercise, think of a time you felt good and there were positive outcomes from the experience. What caused you to feel good (triggering event), what were you thinking at the time, and what was the result?

EMOTION	TRIGGERING EVENT	POSITIVE SELF-TALK	RESULT
1) ________	________________	________________	________________
	________________	________________	________________
	________________	________________	________________
	________________	________________	________________
	________________	________________	________________
	________________	________________	________________

3) For the final part of this exercise, go back to part one. Write down the emotion and triggering event just as you did before, but change your negative self-talk to more positive statements that might help you get out of your painful feelings. Then write what the changed result might turn out to be.

EMOTION	TRIGGERING EVENT	POSITIVE SELF-TALK	RESULT
1) ______	______	______	______
	______	______	______
2) ______	______	______	______
	______	______	______
3) ______	______	______	______
	______	______	______

This exercise can help you understand how you can either make your feelings worse, and thus make the outcome or results worse, or how you can make yourself feel a little better, with better results, depending on how you think and talk to yourself about what is happening. Try it in real life and see how it works. It isn't foolproof, but if you practice changing your thoughts and feelings into more positive ones, you are likely to have a better time in life. Things will go better for you, and you are less likely to fall into destructive or negative ways of acting out your emotions.

Another good exercise for this is the *Thinking Through Emotions Exercise* on the next page. It ties together your feelings, what is happening, how you experience your emotion(s) physically, what you say to yourself, and what happens. Take a blank copy of this sheet with you in your pocket or wallet, and sometime when everything seems to turn out terribly, take it out and fill in the blanks. Answer the questions, then correct your thinking, see what effect it has on your emotions, and how it might have changed the results. This might help you see all the connections and understand the real power you have over yourself, your feelings, your actions, and your life in general.

EXERCISE 19. THINKING THROUGH EMOTIONS

EMOTION What emotion am I feeling?	
SITUATION AND SETTING Where am I? Who am I with? What is happening, or what am I doing?	
SYMPTOMS How am I experiencing the emotion physically?	
THOUGHTS What are my thoughts about what is going on?	
RESULTS Behavior: what do I do or not do as a result?	

CORRECTED THOUGHTS What other ways can I think about what is going on?	
EFFECT ON EMOTIONS What effect do my changed ways of thinking have on my feelings?	
CHANGED RESULTS How could my changed thoughts and feelings affect what I do or don't do in this situation?	

How do emotions fit in with the Offense or Reoffense Chain? It works like this: a *trigger* event starts the whole thing off. Then come thoughts, feelings and behaviors (actions) as shown in the diagram of Jeremiah's Offense Behavior Chain:

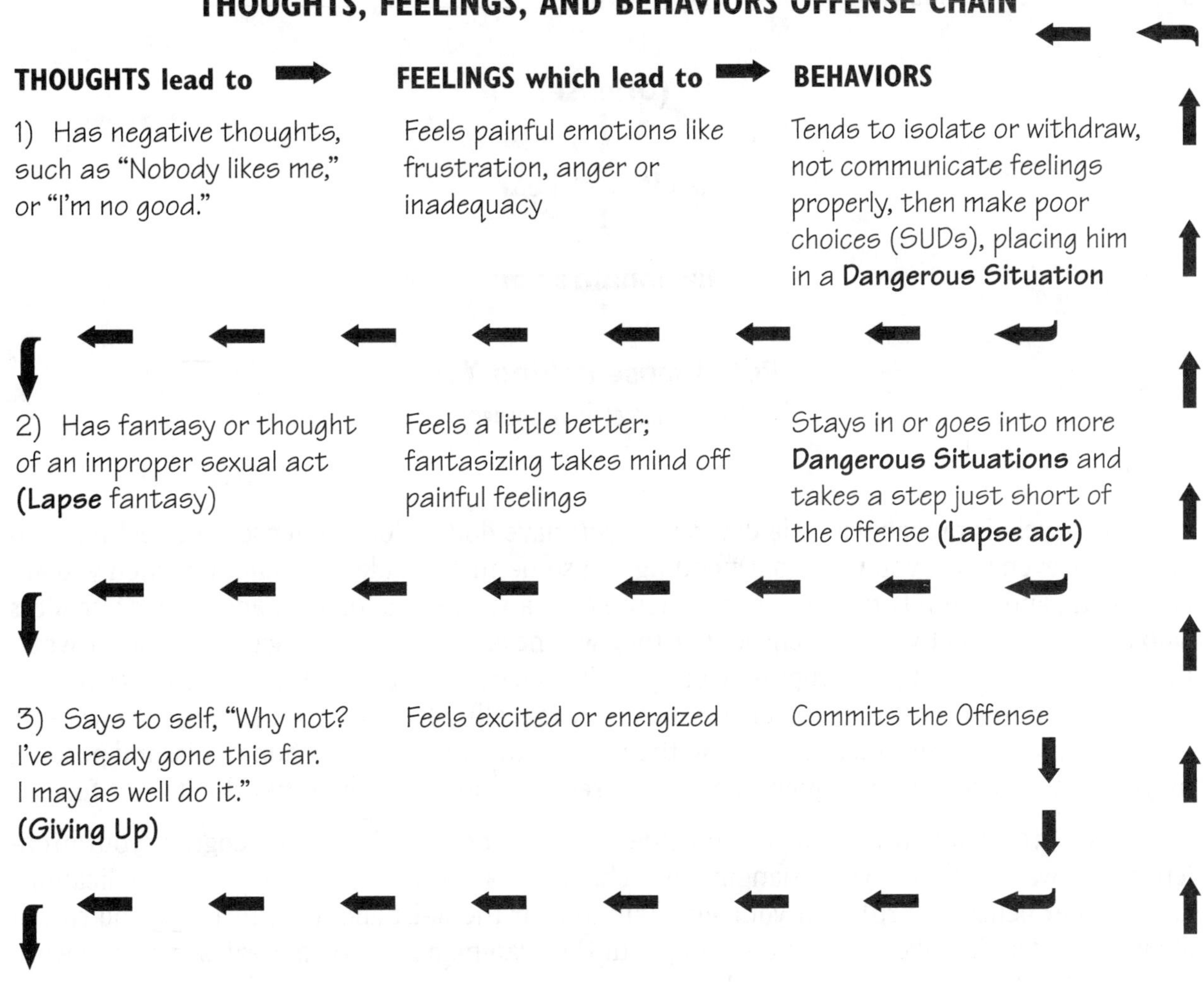

THOUGHTS, FEELINGS, AND BEHAVIORS OFFENSE CHAIN
THOUGHTS lead to
FEELINGS which lead to
BEHAVIORS
1) Has negative thoughts, such as "Nobody likes me," or "I'm no good."
Feels painful emotions like frustration, anger or inadequacy
Tends to isolate or withdraw, not communicate feelings properly, then make poor choices (SUDs), placing him in a Dangerous Situation
2) Has fantasy or thought of an improper sexual act (Lapse fantasy)
Feels a little better; fantasizing takes mind off painful feelings
Stays in or goes into more Dangerous Situations and takes a step just short of the offense (Lapse act)
3) Says to self, "Why not? I've already gone this far. I may as well do it." (Giving Up)
Feels excited or energized
Commits the Offense
4) Thinks, "What have I done? I might get caught. How could I be so stupid?"
After feeling release of tension after offending, feels guilt, fear, and remorse
Goes back to semi-normal activities (and tries to hide thoughts and feelings)

This *Offense Chain* is also called a *Cycle of Offending*, because it can repeat itself unless you are aware of it and take action to change your thoughts, feelings, and behaviors. It can get started at different times, either immediately after an offense when you are feeling badly, after some other triggering event (like being turned down for a date with a someone you really like), or many years down the line when there is a triggering event (like a relationship breakup or loss of job). But you have the power to stop it at any point, just as you can stop your progress down any *Reoffense Chain*.

Did you notice a difference in this chain from the first *Reoffense Chain* you learned? What happens after the offense is committed has been added. After the offense, you may have gotten back to "business as usual," but underneath you probably felt worse about yourself, guilty about the offense, and afraid of what would happen to you. Do you remember feeling that way?

When you are feeling bad, you tend to explain away or rationalize your behavior with thinking errors and distortions (such as, "It's okay, because the same thing happened to me," or "The victim wanted me to do it," or "It won't hurt the victim. He/she will forget about it."). Your guilt and fear begin to fade away, and you try to put your offense behind you. The steps you go through *after* your offense usually look something like this:

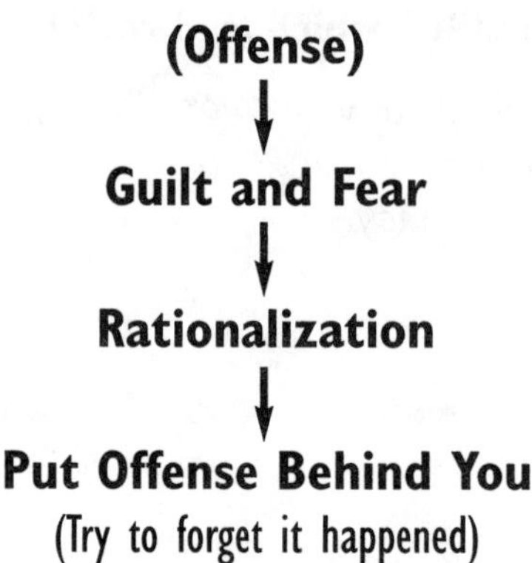

Your cycle is probably a little different if you have done a lot of offenses and feel like you can't stop, even when you want to. Offending can sometimes be like an addiction when you are fantasizing and committing your sexual offense over and over again. Most adolescent offenders who are in treatment want to believe that they will never, never offend again, no matter what. But some adolescents have compulsive or addictive offending patterns; that is, they repeat their offenses over and over again, especially when they're feeling bad or anxious. These adolescents – whose typical offenses include exposing themselves, making obscene phone calls, and peeping in windows – usually have frequent fantasies of reoffending, even when they don't want to.

If you are a compulsive/addictive offender, you may be more likely to recognize your problem and to want to find ways of changing. But changing is harder and you may need medications and tougher behavioral rules for yourself. (Talk to your therapist about medications and rules.) Medications won't make you stop offending, but they can help give you a break so you can work on controlling your out-of-control behavior.

To be safe, all offenders must develop careful plans for themselves not to reoffend. Changing behaviors and thoughts is the first step, understanding and working through emotions is the second. In the pages that follow, you will hopefully understand yourself even better and learn to make better choices.

Review the *Thoughts, Feelings, and Behaviors Offense Chain*, then complete the final exercise of this chapter.

EXERCISE 20. YOUR OWN THOUGHTS, FEELINGS, AND OFFENSE CHAIN

1) What do you think triggered your offense?

2) What thoughts, feelings, and behaviors followed? Record them in the spaces below.

THOUGHTS lead to →	**FEELINGS which lead to** →	**BEHAVIORS**
1) Negative thoughts	Painful emotions	Isolation?
		SUD
		Dangerous Situation
2) Thought or fantasy of offense **(Lapse)**	Feelings when thinking of offending	Further **Dangerous Situation**
		Lapse action
3) **Giving Up** thoughts	Feelings just before offense	**Offense** actions
	At time of offense	
4) Thoughts right after offense	Feelings immediately after offense	What you did right after offense
Later	Later	Later

3) Now think of what you could have done at each of these points to avoid offending. How could you have changed your self-talk? What could you have done to feel better? What *avoidance* and *escape* strategies could you have used to prevent reoffense at each step? Fill in the blanks with offense-prevention strategies.

THOUGHTS lead to →	**FEELINGS which lead to** →	**BEHAVIORS**
1) Change thoughts about self to ___	Things to do about painful emotions	Instead of isolating ___
___	___	**SUD** stage ___
___	___	In a **Dangerous Situation**
___	___	___
___	___	___
___	___	___
___	___	___
2) If thought or fantasy of offense **Lapse**, change to___	What you could do if you ___ still have painful feelings? ___	In a further **Dangerous Situation** ___
___	___	After **Lapse** action ___
___	___	___
___	___	___
___	___	___
___	___	___
3) What to do with ___ **Giving Up** thoughts ___	What to do with painful ___ feelings just before offense ___	Alternatives to **Offense** actions ___
___	___	___
___	___	___
___	___	___
___	___	___
___	___	___

SUMMARY

In this chapter on emotions, you had the opportunity to learn:

1) More words to describe your emotions
2) Increased awareness of what you are feeling at any given time and in any situation
3) More awareness of physical indicators of specific emotions
4) More positive ways of handling and expressing emotions
5) Knowledge of how you can change your emotions through more positive self-talk
6) A better understanding of how both emotions and thoughts affect behavior
7) Knowledge of how thoughts, feelings, and behavior interact in the offense chain, and what to do for a more positive outcome

CHAPTER FIVE

CHOICES

One of the main ideas of Relapse Prevention is that you always have choices – choices as to behavior, thoughts, and even feelings. You have choices whether to act on urges or whether to change your thoughts. You even have a choice about whether or not to come to therapy. You might not like the consequences of not coming to therapy, because your probation officer might report that you have violated your conditions of probation or parole and lock you up. But you have that choice. It's not likely that anyone is going to actually drag you to therapy.

You don't have choices as to consequences, however. They may vary, but you have no control over them. Even so, you can figure out what the likely consequences of your acts will be and act accordingly. You do this all the time without realizing it. When you become aware of the choices you are actually making, you can make better choices that won't lead you closer to reoffending.

There are both positive and negative consequences for all decisions. For example, if you decide to do your homework, the positive consequences are that you will get a better grade in school, receive more teacher approval, feel good about your accomplishment, and maybe even learn something. But the negative consequences are that the work may be painful or boring, you might miss out on some fun time with friends, or you may miss some favorite TV shows or activities. If, on the other hand, you decide *not* to do your homework, there are also positive and negative consequences. The positive consequences are that you will have more fun, not have to suffer through the work, and get to do what you want to do. The negative consequences may include a failing grade, disapproval from your teacher and parents, not understanding what's going on, and feeling stupid in class.

Some consequences are immediate, some are delayed. For example, in the homework situation, not doing the homework may give you immediate pleasure and joy, but later pain and punishment. So we can say that there are short-term and long-term consequences to every decision you make.

In the situation we talked about in Chapter One, where a neighbor in an emergency asked Bill (who had previously molested a child) to babysit, Bill had the choice of saying "yes" or "no." Let us look at the consequences of his initial decision. If he said "no" at the *SUD* (*Seemingly Unimportant Decision*) stage, the main positive consequence is that he would be certain of not reoffending, because he would not be placing himself in a dangerous situation. The negative consequences are that he would be letting down a neighbor in need and might feel mean and unhelpful. On the other hand, if he said "yes," the positive consequences are that he would be helping the neighbor and feel worthwhile. The negative consequences are both short-term (he is now in a place where he is able to commit a sex offense with the neighbor's child) and long-term (he might let down his guard and do even more risky things in a later situation), placing him in a position where he is much more likely to reoffend.

Have you ever made lists of pros and cons, positive and negative results, for decisions you have had to make in the past? Usually people just make two lists – one for the positive consequences or aspects, the other for the negative. In the next exercise, we will be doing this in a little more complex way, a way that can help you see the consequences of your choices more clearly.

Before you do the exercise, look at the example that has been filled in below. Jamal, 15 years old, is trying to decide whether or not to ask Jalissa, a girl he barely knows but would like to know better, to a dance. His choices are to ask her or not to ask her.

POSITIVE AND NEGATIVE CONSEQUENCES SAMPLE CHART

CHOICE	POSITIVE CONSEQUENCES	NEGATIVE CONSEQUENCES
Ask Jalissa to the dance	1) She might say yes. 2) I'd feel great if she said yes. 3) I'd be no worse off if she said no than if I hadn't asked. 4) I'd find out if she liked me. 5) Even if she said no, she might give me some signal that she would go out with me another time.	1) She might turn me down. 2) I'd feel embarrassed and/or rotten if she turned me down. 3) I'd be afraid no girls would like me.
Don't ask Jalissa to the dance	1) I couldn't be turned down. 2) If I got to know her better first, I'd have a better chance of her accepting me. 3) My ego would remain intact. 4) I could still daydream about her liking me, without having to test reality.	1) Maybe she would have gone with me. 2) She might find someone else while I'm trying to get to know her. 3) I may be missing a great time with her. 4) I might never know if she likes me. 5) I'd feel like a chicken.

This gives Jamal a nice clear way to select his options. It is easier to balance the pros and cons when you can see the positive and negative consequences of both doing the act and not doing it. The same chart can be used for different choices, rather than just the choice of doing or not doing a single thing. For example, Jamal might have listed as his choices: asking Jalissa to the dance versus asking her to go to a movie instead, or asking Jalissa to the dance versus asking another girl who he knew likes him and probably would accept. Now try out the positive and negative consequences of a decision you have made in the next exercise.

EXERCISE 21. POSITIVE AND NEGATIVE CONSEQUENCES

Part I) In this part of the exercise, think of a time you had to make a decision (not relating to your offense). What were your two major choices? Write them under "Choice" in the two sections at the left of the chart. Then write down the positive and negative consequences of each.

CHOICE	POSITIVE CONSEQUENCES	NEGATIVE CONSEQUENCES
	1) ______ ______ 2) ______ ______ 3) ______ ______ 4) ______ ______ 5) ______ ______	1) ______ ______ 2) ______ ______ 3) ______ ______ 4) ______ ______ 5) ______ ______
	1) ______ ______ 2) ______ ______ 3) ______ ______ 4) ______ ______ 5) ______ ______	1) ______ ______ 2) ______ ______ 3) ______ ______ 4) ______ ______ 5) ______ ______

Filling out this decision chart can help you understand your decision more clearly. Did you make the right one?

Part 2) This time you make the same analysis of your decision to commit your offense at the point of *Giving Up*, the final step on your offense chain. Look at the consequences of committing your offense versus not committing it. Perhaps if you had weighed out the consequences before your offense, you might have acted differently.

CHOICE	POSITIVE CONSEQUENCES	NEGATIVE CONSEQUENCES
Commit my offense (name your offense)	1) ______ 2) ______ 3) ______ 4) ______ 5) ______	1) ______ 2) ______ 3) ______ 4) ______ 5) ______
Do <u>not</u> commit my offense	1) ______ 2) ______ 3) ______ 4) ______ 5) ______	1) ______ 2) ______ 3) ______ 4) ______ 5) ______

You can do this exercise at each step of your offense chain. You can make it more detailed by dividing the consequences into short-term and long-term. The chart on the next page does just that.

Part 3) In this part, think back to your own *SUD (Seemingly Unimportant Decision)*. In the top section, write down what your choice was. On the bottom, write another choice you could have made instead. Then, fill in the short and long term positive and negative consequences of each.

SHORT AND LONG TERM CONSEQUENCES

CHOICE	SHORT TERM CONSEQUENCES		LONG TERM CONSEQUENCES	
	POSITIVE	NEGATIVE	POSITIVE	NEGATIVE
SUD: ____ What I did ____	1) ____ 2) ____ 3) ____ 4) ____ 5) ____	1) ____ 2) ____ 3) ____ 4) ____ 5) ____	1) ____ 2) ____ 3) ____ 4) ____ 5) ____	1) ____ 2) ____ 3) ____ 4) ____ 5) ____
SUD: ____ What I could have done instead ____	1) ____ 2) ____ 3) ____ 4) ____ 5) ____	1) ____ 2) ____ 3) ____ 4) ____ 5) ____	1) ____ 2) ____ 3) ____ 4) ____ 5) ____	1) ____ 2) ____ 3) ____ 4) ____ 5) ____

You can also use this system with thoughts and feelings as well as behavior. In the next section of this exercise, you will have the opportunity to try this.

Part 4) Pick a time when you felt "put-down" by someone. It could be a parent, other family member, teacher, or friend. What was that situation? Write it here. ______________________________

Think about a positive statement (positive self-talk) you could have made to yourself at that moment. Then think of a negative statement (negative self-talk). Write both down below. What would the consequences have been? Note that the consequences can be feelings, not just happenings.

CHOICE	POSITIVE CONSEQUENCES	NEGATIVE CONSEQUENCES
Positive self-talk statement: ______	1) ______ 2) ______ 3) ______ 4) ______	1) ______ 2) ______ 3) ______ 4) ______
Negative self-talk statement: ______	1) ______ 2) ______ 3) ______ 4) ______	1) ______ 2) ______ 3) ______ 4) ______

As you have seen, at each point along your offense chain, you had the opportunity to make choices. Any time you choose to think, act, or feel a certain way, there are positive and negative consequences. If you make yourself aware of the consequences, you have the opportunity to make different, healthier choices. You have the power to find different ways of looking at things, different ways to act, and different ways to feel based on what you say to yourself. You have the power of *choice*.

In the next exercise, you have the opportunity to look at some poor choices.

EXERCISE 22. CHANGING POOR CHOICES

Read the following scenarios. Write down all of the poor choices that Franco and Elizabeth made, starting from the beginning. Then write down what better choices they could have made.

1) Franco, age 15, just got out of a juvenile detention facility for molesting a neighbor child. At 3:00 p.m., he felt hungry. Since there was nothing he wanted to eat in the refrigerator at home, he decided to walk to the store. The shortest way was to cut through the schoolyard, so he walked that way. A 6-year-old girl was looking for her ball. He saw it in the bushes, so he took her to it. She said she was hungry, so he offered to buy her some food at the store if she would wait for him. He went to the store. A small boy was crying in the back of the store, because he couldn't find his mother. Franco gave the boy a piece of gum and the child stopped crying. He told the child to come with him and he would find the mother. The mother came along just then, so he paid for what he had taken and left the store. On the way out, he stopped to talk to a group of young children. They asked him if he would coach their basketball team. He said yes and agreed to meet with them the following day. He left then to take the food he bought to the child he had met in the schoolyard.

There are at least 9 or 10 poor choices Franco made here. List them in the first column. Include thoughts, feelings, and behaviors. Then list the better choices he could have made in the second column.

POOR CHOICE	BETTER CHOICE
1) ______________________	______________________
______________________	______________________
2) ______________________	______________________
______________________	______________________
3) ______________________	______________________
______________________	______________________
4) ______________________	______________________
______________________	______________________
5) ______________________	______________________
______________________	______________________
6) ______________________	______________________
______________________	______________________
7) ______________________	______________________
______________________	______________________
8) ______________________	______________________
______________________	______________________
9) ______________________	______________________
______________________	______________________

2) Elizabeth was on probation for molesting her younger sister Courtney. She was required to live at her grandmother's, away from home. Nobody was home and Elizabeth felt very lonesome. Last Thursday, she called home to talk to her mother during the day even though her mother usually was still at work. Courtney answered the phone. She told Courtney how sorry she was about what she had done, how much she loved and missed her, and how much she would like to be able to talk to Courtney in person. Courtney said she would come over on the bus. When she got there, Elizabeth invited her into the house. They sat down on the sofa and talked for a while. Elizabeth began to think about how loving and warm it would be to touch her sister's body. Elizabeth asked if she could hug Courtney, because Elizabeth felt so lonely. Courtney agreed. In the process of hugging, Elizabeth's hand accidentally rubbed against her sister's breast. Courtney didn't say anything. Elizabeth figured, "Since I've gone this far and she doesn't mind, I may as well touch the rest of her." She acted on these thoughts, committing another sex offense.

In this scenario, there are about 10 or 11 poor choices Elizabeth made. What are they? Include thoughts, feelings and behaviors. What better choices could Elizabeth have made?

POOR CHOICE	**BETTER CHOICE**
1) ______________________	______________________
______________________	______________________
2) ______________________	______________________
______________________	______________________
3) ______________________	______________________
______________________	______________________
4) ______________________	______________________
______________________	______________________
5) ______________________	______________________
______________________	______________________
6) ______________________	______________________
______________________	______________________
7) ______________________	______________________
______________________	______________________
8) ______________________	______________________
______________________	______________________
9) ______________________	______________________
______________________	______________________

3) Look again at Elizabeth's situation. Which of Elizabeth's behaviors were *SUDs*? What were the *Dangerous Situations* she placed herself in? How did she *Lapse*? What did say to herself that was *Giving Up*? Write each of those in the spaces below. (Notice the increasingly dangerous situations Elizabeth put herself in by her poor choices and that she lapsed both in thought and behavior.)

SUD (Seemingly Unimportant Decision) ______________________

____

____

Dangerous Situation ______________________

____

____

____

Lapse(s) (Thought and/or action bringing Elizabeth very close to offending) ______________________

____

____

____

____

____

Giving Up ____

____

____

____

____

____

Offense: Touching her sister's private parts.

Can you see how Elizabeth may not have been aware of where her initial actions were leading, or thought she had everything under control? How she may not have been aware of the choices she was making?

One of your treatment goals is to become more conscious of your choices and decisions. Arms and legs do not move without your choosing to make them move. Sex offenses don't just happen. You made a series of decisions and chose to commit your offense. Even if you allowed a younger child to do something to you, that was a choice you made. As we said at the beginning of this chapter, if you are more conscious of your choices and their consequences, you are more likely to make good choices, choices that won't get you into trouble. So think first, and think things through before you act.

Another way to make good choices is to look at some of the reasons why you made the past choices you did. Most people who make poor choices do it in order to meet their emotional needs, although they've chosen negative ways to do that. Elizabeth's choice to reoffend was a negative way to deal with her loneliness and need to feel loved. Franco's may have been because he felt crummy about himself and wanted to be liked and looked up to. Both of them chose to satisfy their needs in ways that were dangerous for them and for the children they were with.

For all the needs you have, there are negative and positive ways to satisfy them; the positive ways are ones that won't lead you down the *Offense Chain*. For example, Elizabeth could have called her mother at work or her counselor or a friend, she could have gone over to a friend's house, she could have run at the track or gone to a movie, she could have written a poem or drawn a picture about her loneliness, or she could have talked herself into feeling better, like saying, "This loneliness will pass. I can do something positive for myself right now that will make me feel better."

In the next exercise, we will look at some needs that people try to satisfy by offending, and find better alternatives to satisfy those needs.

EXERCISE 23. NEEDS SATISFACTION

1) Cover up the second part of this exercise. (Come on, don't cheat!) We want you to think for yourself. On the following lines, write down what needs you think you were trying to satisfy when you committed your offense(s). Brainstorm as many as you can ______________________________

2) In the left-hand column on the next page, we have listed some of the common needs that sex offenders are trying to fill when they commit their sex offenses. In the middle column, list ways that you have tried to meet these needs that were unhealthy for you and/or harmed someone else and got you into trouble. In the right-hand column, fill in other, healthier ways you could and/or would fill those needs if you had them. Include specific actions or activities you might do. For example, if your need was for power and control, maybe one of your ways of satisfying this need would be to play football. List at least three alternatives for each need.

NEEDS BEHIND SEX OFFENSES	NEGATIVE WAYS I'VE MET THIS NEED	BETTER WAYS OF SATISFYING THEM
Power or control	1) ______	1) ______
(feeling helpless,	2) ______	2) ______
out of control)	3) ______	3) ______
Excitement (feeling	1) ______	1) ______
bored, life is dull)	2) ______	2) ______
	3) ______	3) ______
Caring, connection, or	1) ______	1) ______
love (feeling lonely)	2) ______	2) ______
	3) ______	3) ______
To be looked up to, admired,	1) ______	1) ______
respected, or thought capa-	2) ______	2) ______
ble (feeling inadequate)	3) ______	3) ______
To release or vent anger	1) ______	1) ______
(feeling frustrated or	2) ______	2) ______
angry)	3) ______	3) ______
Sexual satisfaction, or to	1) ______	1) ______
fulfill sexual fantasy	2) ______	2) ______
(feeling sexual)	3) ______	3) ______
To feel whole, or like your	1) ______	1) ______
life has some purpose	2) ______	2) ______
(feeling empty inside)	3) ______	3) ______
Other need (you name)	1) ______	1) ______
	2) ______	2) ______
	3) ______	3) ______
Other need (you name)	1) ______	1) ______
	2) ______	2) ______
	3) ______	3) ______

You are going to have urges, fantasies, or opportunities to offend in the future, even if you feel sure now that you will never have them again. Having urges, fantasies and opportunities to offend doesn't make you a bad person. It is what you do with these urges, fantasies and opportunities that counts.

A final skill related to making good choices is *Problem Solving.* Every problem has lots of solutions. Some of these solutions are better than others, based on the consequences that happen afterward. Once again, no solutions are all negative or all positive. There are positive and negative consequences to each.

When you have a problem, it is a good idea to brainstorm lots of solutions. Make a long list.

If you have friends who can help, make them part of the process. After you make your list, cross out the impossible or clearly negative solutions. Look carefully at the ones you have left. Which ones seem to be the better ones? Will you be able to use any of them? What are the likely consequences of each? Think this over carefully. Finally pick the best one. (You can also use your Chart of Positive and Negative Consequences in Exercise 21 to think though the results.)

In the following exercise, you will have the opportunity to generate a variety of solutions to problems, and then to choose the best one. For example, if Walt wants to go to the movies next Friday, but doesn't have the money now, what are some possible solutions?

1) Borrow money from a friend

2) Ask employer for an advance

3) Ask employer if he can work overtime

4) Not go

5) Ask neighbors if they need some yardwork done at a reasonable price

EXERCISE 24. PROBLEM SOLVING

For the following problems, write down at least four different solutions. Then, after thinking of the likely consequences, in the left hand margin, place a check in front of the solution you think would be the best one.

1) Lee got an F on his algebra test. He doesn't understand the material. What can he do?

a) ______

b) ______

c) ______

d) ______

2) Donna loaned her tape recorder to her friend Jack. Jack lost it. What should Donna do if Jack doesn't replace it?

a) ______

b) ______

c) ______

d) ______

3) Abe's brother always puts him down. Abe would like this to change. What can he do?

a) ______

b) ______

c) ______

d) ______

4) Juan disrespected Luis's mother in front of his friends. What can Luis do about this?

a) ____________________

b) ____________________

c) ____________________

d) ____________________

5) Neal likes Janice. He wants to know if she likes him. What can he do to find out?

a) ____________________

b) ____________________

c) ____________________

d) ____________________

6) Andre is being pressured to join a gang. Gangs rule his school and neighborhood. He wants to be safe, but he doesn't want to be part of a gang. What can he do?

a) ____________________

b) ____________________

c) ____________________

d) ____________________

7) Bill just got grounded for the week for not doing his chores. He had finally gotten a date to go to the senior prom this Saturday night with Colleen, a girl he has wanted to ask out all year. What should/could he do?

a) ____________________

b) ____________________

c) ____________________

d) ____________________

8) Lola has been going out with someone she's wanted to date for a long time. He is pressuring her to have sex, but she doesn't feel ready yet. She is afraid of losing him if she doesn't give in. What can she do?

a) ____________________

b) ____________________

c) ____________________

d) ____________________

9) Steve's parents are very strict. All his friends get to come home at midnight on the weekends, but his parents make him come home at 10:00 p.m. There is going to be a big party this weekend. Steve wants to go and stay until midnight. What can he do?

a) ____________________

b) ____________________

c) ____________________

d) ____________________

10) Jake is being physically abused by his father. He wants it to stop, but doesn't want his father to get into trouble or leave the home. What can he do?

a) ______

b) ______

c) ______

d) ______

11) Penny's parents get drunk and violent every weekend. This really upsets her. What can she do?

a) ______

b) ______

c) ______

d) ______

12) Rob is being molested by his older brother and his brother's friends. He loves his older brother, but wants the sexual abuse to stop. What can he do?

a) ______

b) ______

c) ______

d) ______

13) Sam has dyslexia and can't read. He is smart, so he has been hiding it for years. He would like to learn to read, but doesn't want anyone to know he can't read. What can he do?

a) ______

b) ______

c) ______

d) ______

14) Luke's best friend Matt talks about everything to everyone. He tells others Luke's secrets. How can Luke remain best friends with Matt but get him to shut up?

a) ______

b) ______

c) ______

d) ______

15) Abe is a senior in high school. He plans to go on to college. He just found out that his girlfriend Marilyn is pregnant. He wants her to get an abortion, but she doesn't believe in it. What can he do now?

a) ______

b) ______

c) ______

d) ______

16) Eddie didn't study for his history midterm. He just found out that he won't be able to play football if he doesn't get a B on the exam. What can he do?

a) ______

b) ______

c) ______________________________

d) ______________________________

17) Kent realizes he has a drug problem and can't seem to kick it by himself. He is afraid to tell his parents. What can he do?

a) ______________________________

b) ______________________________

c) ______________________________

d) ______________________________

18) Pete's step-dad, who just got out of prison, has all kinds of stolen property in the house. Pete's mom needs the step-dad there to support the family. Pete is on probation and is afraid that if the police or his probation officer find out about the stuff, they will blame him. What can he do?

a) ______________________________

b) ______________________________

c) ______________________________

d) ______________________________

19) Linda's mother is in jail. None of her friends know. Linda is embarrassed about it. There is a mother-daughter event at school and all Linda's friends and their mothers are going. Linda has to give a speech there. What should she do or say about her missing mother?

a) ______________________________

b) ______________________________

c) ______________________________

d) ______________________________

As you can see, often there is no solution that is really good in these situations. Sometimes it is necessary to compromise on the best of bad solutions. But there are always choices available, and some are better than others. Looking at the probable consequences of each and balancing them is a way of finding what is likely to work the best.

SUMMARY

What you could have gained from this chapter:

1) Awareness that you have choices in almost every one of your acts, thoughts, or emotions
2) Awareness that each choice you make has positive and negative consequences
3) Knowledge about different ways of weighing the consequences of your choices
4) An understanding of how choices fit in your *Offense Chain*
5) An understanding of how your needs underlie the choices you make
6) Increased awareness of the needs that were behind your own offense
7) Awareness that you have many choices in fulfilling your needs
8) Recognition of choices in problem solving and ways to make better choices

NOTES

CHAPTER SIX

URGE CONTROL

You have already learned to *Avoid* and *Escape* from dangerous situations, and you have learned that you can change your thoughts, but what about your physical urges? Sexual urges, like any other bodily urges (hunger, urination, and so forth) do not have to be satisfied to go away. After a while, they gradually vanish by themselves. Think of urges like waves, going up and down naturally.

This is important information, because it means that you can wait out your urges or do something else until your urge subsides. You have a *choice* whether or not to act on your urge, and if you decide to act, you can choose whether or not that act will be healthy or unhealthy

There are also urges that come from your emotional needs, but may be translated into physical urges. For example, when you are feeling bored and lonely, you may have the urge to eat, even if you aren't physically hungry. You may have eaten just an hour before, but you crave some cookies. You remember the pleasure cookies gave you in the past and are attempting to capture that pleasure again. You don't even think about the negative consequences – how you will gain unwanted weight or spoil your appetite for dinner. You just grab more and more of them and wolf them down.

This need to satisfy an emotional need is called the *Problem of Immediate Gratification*, abbreviated simply to *PIG*. The PIG also applies to sexual urges. If you have been feeling some painful emotions, such as depression or anger, you may crave the sexual act you committed, because you remember the pleasure or release it gave you.

For example, some kids at school made fun of Yoshi. He felt depressed, unliked and stupid. He was walking home through the park when he saw a little boy standing by a tree. Yoshi had the urge to touch the child's penis. This is the PIG. If Yoshi did this before to try to feel better, he is more likely repeat the behavior. The PIG fits its name. It is a greedy animal. It wants to be fed over and over again. The more you give in to it, the more you crave that sexual release.

Before you can handle your PIG, you have to become aware of it and what gets it going. Recognizing the painful emotions and negative thinking that trigger the PIG, then becoming aware of the cravings or urges before you act on them are the first steps.

Using what you have learned earlier in this book can help you avoid feeding the PIG. These skills include 1) using *Avoidance* and *Escape* techniques to prevent you from going down your *Offense Chain*; 2) changing your negative thoughts and self-talk to more positive ones; and 3) finding more positive ways of satisfying your needs.

You don't have to wait until you feel the urge. You can plan ahead. You can avoid getting into high risk situations. You can do things that put you in a more positive state of mind. Getting plenty of sleep, exercising, and eating well all help you avoid the PIG.

If you are already having the urge or craving for an inappropriate sexual activity, you still do not have to act on it. There are a few ways you can help yourself stop. First, you can make an

Urge Control Contract of what you will do instead of or before acting on an urge.Second, you can carry a card with you at all times and read it to help you either to wait out the urge or make yourself safe.

The following are samples of an *Urge Control Contract* and an *Urge Control Card*.

URGE CONTROL CONTRACT

I, Dana Holly, recognize that I may sometimes have urges or fantasies to reoffend. I know that I am a valuable human being who cares about others, so I am making this contract as an insurance policy against reoffending. I hereby promise that when I have an urge, fantasy, or opportunity to commit a sex offense or any act close to an offense, I will do as much of the following as possible:

1) Stop or change my dangerous sexual fantasies by yelling STOP to myself and substituting a negative fantasy of being arrested or humiliated at school.
2) Tell myself it is not worth taking any chances, I can **avoid** or **escape** a dangerous situation, it is never too late until the deed is done, and I can succeed in **not** offending.
3) Write out a good and bad consequences chart about reoffending or not reoffending.
4) Think about what needs I am trying to satisfy through offending and try to find some other ways of satisfying them.
5) Change what I am doing to something safe that will take my mind off offending.
6) Read my **Urge Control Card.**
7) Talk to a friend, counselor, or probation officer or call a crisis hotline (such as child abuse, rape crisis, and so forth).
8) Go someplace where I cannot offend (to someone else's house, to the police or probation department, and so forth).
9) If I still feel the urge and these alternatives aren't possible, take 40 deep breaths, exhaling slowly.
10) If none of these techniques work, wait at least 20 minutes to allow the urge to go away.

Afterward, I will talk to my group and/or counselor about having the urge or fantasy, what I think were the causes behind it, and what I did to successfully overcome it. I will also reward myself for successfully following my contract by doing something positive I enjoy (like going to a sports event, concert, bowling, or movie).

I agree to read this plan over every Sunday night as a reminder to keep myself safe.

Signed: Dana Holly

Dated: September 25, 1993

URGE CONTROL CARD

When I get a strong fantasy, thought, or urge to commit a sex offense, I will sit down and carefully read over the following:

1) A fantasy, thought, or urge to reoffend is not unusual. It doesn't mean I have lost control or failed. And it doesn't mean I have to offend.

2) If I feel scared or guilty about my sexual fantasy, thought and/or urge, I will remind myself that I have power over them. I don't have to give in to them. I have other choices. I have other options that can satisfy my needs besides offending.

3) I will think of this as a learning experience. I will look at my life and try to figure out what has led up to the fantasy, thought, or urge. I will try to figure out what need I am trying to satisfy, and I will brainstorm all the other positive ways I can meet my needs.

4) If I am still having trouble, I will think about who I can call to talk to. I will look at the phone numbers of these resources on the other side of this card and call until I can talk to one of them.

Name and phone number of friend: Lee – 555-7913

Name and phone number of therapist: Sara Johnson
555-3629

Name and phone number of probation officer Mr. Frank Jacobs
555-4850

Hotline phone number Suicide Helpline – 555-1111

Above all, I will remind myself that I am in control.
An urge or fantasy does not make me a sex offender.
I am in control. This urge will pass.

Now it is time for you to make your own *Urge Control Card*. Copy the card above exactly on a 3" by 5" index card, fill in the names and phone numbers, and carry it with you at all times in your wallet. Don't forget you have it there.

Your next exercise is to make up your own *Urge Control Contract*. You can use the format suggested below or change it to suit your own situation. Fill in your own name, your own negative fantasy, your own reward, and your own times to reread the contract. Also specify what places are safe and who you will call to talk to or ask for help. Make sure you have more than one person to call plus a local hotline. The hotlines are important, because you are sure to reach someone all the time. Then sign and date your contract. Remember: this is a way you can help protect yourself.

EXERCISE 25. MY URGE CONTROL CONTRACT

I,____, recognize that I may sometimes have urges, fantasies, or opportunities to reoffend. I know that I am a valuable human being who cares about others, so I am making this contract as an insurance policy against reoffending. I hereby promise that when I have an urge, fantasy, or opportunity to commit a sex offense or any act close to an offense I will do as much of the following as possible:

1) Stop or change my dangerous sexual fantasies by yelling stop to myself and substituting a fantasy of

____

2) Tell myself it is not worth taking any chances, I can avoid or escape a dangerous situation, it is never too late until the deed is done, and I can succeed in not offending.

3) Write out a positive and negative consequences chart about reoffending or not reoffending.

4) Think about what needs I am trying to satisfy through offending and try to find some other ways of satisfying them.

5) Change what I am doing to something safe that will take my mind off of offending.

6) Read my Urge Control Card.

7) Talk to (friend and/or relative)____________________________________,

____

(counselor) ____

or (probation officer)____________________________________,

or call the ____hotline.

8) Go to one of the following places where I cannot offend:

a)____,

b)____,

or c) ____.

9) If I still feel the urge, I will take 40 deep breaths, exhaling slowly.

10) If none of the above work, I will wait at least 20 minutes to allow the urge to go away.

Afterward, I will talk to my group and/or counselor about having the urge or fantasy, what I think were the causes behind it, and what I did to successfully overcome it. I will also reward myself for successfully following my contract by

____

____

I agree to read this plan every________________________as a reminder to keep myself safe.

Signed ______________________________ Dated________________

So you now have a plan for coping with your fantasies, urges, or opportunities to offend. But how about coping with *emotions* that get you into trouble, like anger? You can make a plan regarding that emotion, much like the *Urge Control Contract*. In it, you can promise yourself to notice how you are feeling physically, so you will recognize that emotion coming on, and have various healthy alternative outlets planned in advance. Again, it is important to reward yourself for using the healthy outlets and to schedule a time for rereading the contract. A sample anger plan is shown below:

SAMPLE ANGER PLAN

This is Dana Holly's anger contract, which Dana has made to prevent Dana from inappropriately expressing anger.

A. I recognize that I usually am thinking the following things before my anger develops:

1) I think I am being picked on unfairly.
2) I feel that I am not liked or respected.
3) I feel misunderstood.

B. I feel the following bodily cues that tell me I am angry:

1) My muscles tense, particularly my face muscles.
2) My voice gets louder and aggressive.
3) My breathing is faster and shallower.
4) I tend to pace.
5) My energy increases.

C. I will observe the following plan when I am getting angry:

1) I will take a time-out or leave the place where my anger has come on and go to a safe place.
2) I will try to change my self-talk to something more positive.
3) I will talk to a friend, counselor, probation officer, or family member about how I am feeling.
4) When I cool down, I will either tell or write a note to the person with whom I am angry about what I felt and why.
5) I will talk about my anger in group.

D. I will keep a journal of my angry feelings with the date, what the situation was, and rate the level of anger from 1 (slight) to 10 (extreme).

E. If I did not follow this plan, I will give myself a negative consequence by not allowing myself to watch TV that night.

F. If I followed this plan, I will reward myself by playing basketball this week.

G. I will review this plan every Monday morning before I go to school.

Signed: Dated:

September 25, 1993

Dana Holly

Now it is your turn to make a plan for a particular emotion with which you have had problems. Follow the outline in Exercise 26.

EXERCISE 26. MY EMOTION PLAN

BEHAVIOR ADDRESSED: Inappropriate expression of (name emotion)____________________

____

NEGATIVE SELF-TALK (NEGATIVE THOUGHTS) CREATING THIS FEELING:

1) ____________________

2) ____________________

3) ____________________

PHYSICAL CUES TO HELP ME IDENTIFY THE EMOTION:

1) ____________________

3) ____________________

2) ____________________

4) ____________________

PLAN – THINGS I WILL DO TO MAKE SURE I DEAL IN A HEALTHY WAY WITH THE EMOTION: (Include who you will talk to)

1) ____________________

2) ____________________

3) ____________________

4) ____________________

RECORD OF THE EMOTION (JOURNAL OR DIAGRAM, AND WHAT IT WILL INCLUDE):

____

____

____

SELF-IMPOSED NEGATIVE CONSEQUENCES FOR NOT FOLLOWING PLAN:

____

SELF-REWARD FOR FOLLOWING PLAN:

____

REREADING OF PLAN:

I will reread this plan (when and where) ____________________

Signed: ____________________ Date: __________

None of your plans will help you handle your emotions unless you reread your plans frequently and follow them regularly. All training, whether for football or learning multiplication tables, takes time and effort. But when you think of the negative consequences if you don't change some of your problem areas, the time and effort you invest will be well worth it.

SUMMARY

In this chapter you had the opportunity to learn:

1) About the ups and downs of urges
2) How to deal with the *Problem of Immediate Gratification (PIG)*
3) How to write an *Urge Control Contract*
4) How to make an *Urge Control Card*
5) How to develop an *Emotion Plan* to deal with painful emotions

NOTES

NOTES

CHAPTER SEVEN

UNDERSTANDING YOURSELF

In the preceding chapters, we looked at behaviors, thoughts, and emotions in a very technical way. Now is the time to more personally look at *you*, who *you* are, and what *you* have experienced, thought, and felt. It is a time to bring up painful past memories, work through rather than ignore the feelings that resulted, and find out more about the person inside you.

Why is this important to preventing reoffending? Because until *you* come to terms with yourself, fully open up your emotions, resolve the issues that contribute to your offending, and build healthy self-esteem, you are at high risk of reoffense. In addition, you cannot possibly understand what your victims have felt if you don't understand and feel *your own* emotional responses.

A good starting place is to take an inventory of yourself. The inventory can help you see the many different sides of yourself, both on the outside and inside. What do you look like? How do you think? What do you feel about yourself and the world? Where do family and friends fit in? What are your goals, desires, and needs?

The exercise below gives you a format for a self-inventory. It is in no way complete, but you may begin to see yourself more clearly after you have described yourself in detail.

EXERCISE 27. SELF-INVENTORY

1) **General Information**:

Name____________________ Age________ Sex______

2) **Physical Characteristics**:

Weight________ Height________ Eyes________ Figure/Physique ________

Hair: Color________ Do you like your hair? ________________

Is it (circle answer): Natural/Dyed? Short/Long? Curly/Straight?

Appearance: How would you describe yourself? (Look in the mirror if necessary and select and write your answe from the following words: "very," "quite," "somewhat," or "not.")

Attractive ________	Ugly ________	Physically Fit________
Large________	Small ________	Fat ________
Well-coordinated ________	Clumsy________	Ordinary ________
Unusual ________	Sloppy ________	Well-groomed ________
Casual ________	Weird ________	Skinny ________
Muscular ________	Weak________	Graceful ________

How else would you describe your body? ________________

How do you usually dress (conservative, grunge, wild, etc?) ____________________

What is your favorite feature?____________________

Do others appreciate your appearance?__________ Who?____________________

3) **Mind**: Which words or phrases describe your mental processes? (Select and write your answer from the following words: "very," "generally," "sometimes," or "not.")

School smart __________ Street smart__________ Sharp (quick) __________

Bright __________ Stupid __________ Talented __________

Clever __________ Deep thinking__________ Capable__________

Funny __________ Sophisticated __________ Imaginative __________

Mature __________ Childish __________ Aware__________

Naive (trusting, believing, unworldly)____________________

Good sense of humor____________________

Creative__________(at what?)____________________

What do you like most about your mind?____________________

Do others appreciate your mind?__________ Who? ____________________

4) **Feelings**: Describe your feelings by writing in one of the following words: "very," "generally," "somewhat," or not."

Happy __________ Sad/Depressed__________ Angry__________

Frustrated __________ Strong __________ Weak __________

Emotional __________ Nervous/Anxious __________ Lonely __________

Loved__________ Well-liked __________ Independent __________

Needy __________ Bored __________ Lively__________

Self-centered__________ Caring of others __________ Unfeeling__________

Explosive__________ Calm __________ Tired __________

Serious __________ Light-hearted __________ Fearless__________

Scared __________ Self-confident __________ Insecure __________

Are there any other feeling words that would describe you? ____________________

____

____

What do you like most about the way you feel? ____________________

____

Are there ways you would rather feel? How? ____________________

____

Do others appreciate the good ways you feel?__________ Who?____________________

What do they appreciate? ____________________

Describe some times when you really felt good? ____________________

____

5) **Behavior**: How would you describe your general behavior? (Select and write your answer from the following words: "usually," "often," "sometimes," or "not.")

Obedient ____	Respectful ____	Conservative ____
Wild ____	Irresponsible ____	"Cool" ____
Flashy ____	Ready to fight ____	Friendly ____
Aggressive ____	Stand up for self ____	Stand up for others ____
Daring ____	Honest ____	Trustworthy ____
Loner ____	Self sufficient ____	Sexy ____
Cheap ____	Classy ____	Defiant ____
Leader ____	Do what others want ____	Overly responsible ____
Cruel ____	Kind ____	User ____
Impulsive ____	Compulsive ____	Impatient ____
Loser ____	Winner ____	Good at sports ____
Good in school ____	Good lover ____	Good friend ____
Good worker ____	Enjoy playing around ____	Tease ____
Gossip ____	Can keep secrets ____	Talk back ____
Fight a lot ____	Steal ____	Cheat ____

Take or do what I want no matter what effect it has on others ____

What other words or phrases describe your behavior? ____

____

6) **Family**: Describe your family by writing in one of the following words: "mostly," "somewhat," "a little," or "not." (Include natural and step-parents, natural and step-brothers and sisters, grandparents or other relatives who also live with you, and adoptive parents. Do not include foster family members.)

Close ____	Distant ____	Important to me ____
Trustworthy ____	Well-adjusted ____	Dysfunctional ____
There for me ____	Not available ____	Good listeners ____
Rigid ____	Flexible ____	Smothering ____
Shaming ____	Hurtful ____	Mean ____
Abusive ____	Fair ____	Respectful ____
Embarrassing ____	Fun to be with ____	Boring ____
Caring ____	Smart ____	Stupid ____
Cruel ____	Insensitive ____	Loyal ____
Chaotic ____	Calm ____	Fun ____
Intellectual ____	Good at sports ____	Mechanical ____
Artistic ____	Clever ____	Angry ____

Law Abiding ____ Lawbreakers (who?) ____

Religious ____ Alcoholic (who?) ____

Successful____________________ Drug users (who?) ____________________

Do any of your family members come to you for help or a listening ear? Who?____________________

Are you a lot like any of your family members? If yes, who?____________________

Are you very different from most of the others? How?____________________

How would you change your family if you could? ____________________

____

____

7) **Your Life**: What is important to you? (Select and write your answer from the following words: "very," "quite," "somewhat," or "not.")

Friends __________	School __________	Being in a group __________
Being liked __________	Being independent __________	Being popular __________
Affection __________	Love __________	Sex __________
Sports __________	Music __________	Other arts __________
Creativity __________	Building or making things _____	Knowledge __________
Money __________	Possessions __________	Travel __________
Career __________	Freedom __________	Rules __________
Being unique __________	Blending in __________	Partying __________
Personal growth __________	Politics __________	Security __________
Excitement __________	Variety __________	Consistency __________

Other things ____

What are you currently doing to get most of the things above that are important to you? __________

____

____

Are there things you could do to get the important things but aren't? What?____________________

____

____

What seems to get in the way or stop you? ____________________

____

____

____

8) **Analysis**: Carefully read all you have written above. See how it all fits together. You may have a little better picture of yourself, who you are, how you think, feel, and act, your roots, and what is important to you in life.

What would you like to change? ____________________

____

____

____

What can you do to improve these things? (You may not be able to totally change some, but you often can make improvements, especially in your own thoughts, feelings and behaviors.)____________________

9) **Goals**: For this last section, think of an imaginary but possible scenario describing your life as you would like it to be 10 years from now. Then write your answers to these questions:

Where will you be living? __________

Who with? __________

Will you be married or in a relationship? __________

Will you have children?__________

Will you have pets or stock animals?__________

How much education will you have? __________

What work will you do? __________

What will your money situation be? __________

How will you have fun?__________

What kind of social life will you have?__________

What kinds of projects will you do or be part of? __________

What kinds of relationships will you have? __________

Where and how will you travel?__________

What will your spiritual life be like? __________

How will you be helping others? __________

What will your most important possessions be?__________

Other? __________

Think of these as your *goals*. Goals are simply what you want your life to be like. You can achieve almost all of them if you put your energies toward the steps to attain them. Writing these 16 or more goals out separately on a piece of paper or card and tacking them up somewhere where you will look at them frequently is a good idea. It is important not to forget about them. You may at times modify them, as your desires change and as time goes on. But always keep them in the back of your mind, and think about them as you make decisions that will affect your life. By setting realistic goals and making good decisions, your life will have some direction, and you are less likely to act foolishly or self-destructively.

When you were caught after committing a sex offense, you probably thought of yourself as a pretty terrible person, even though you may have shrugged off the offense on the outside. You probably would be totally mad at anyone who did what you did, especially if the victim was someone you cared about. Even if you molested a younger brother or sister you don't get along with, you would be mad if someone else did the same thing. You might even feel like you would attack someone who had sexually assaulted your girlfriend or boyfriend or a family member. And if you did things like exposing yourself, peeping in windows, making obscene phone calls, or other illegal sexual acts, you probably secretly think of yourself as a weird and sick person.

(If you think of your behavior as perfectly okay, it simply means that you are out of touch with your feelings toward yourself and toward others. You will have to work harder uncovering those feelings – bringing them into awareness. We will do more work on feelings toward yourself in the material that follows.)

You are *not* a bad person. You do have a problem. You have done some bad things, you did hurt your victim (perhaps severely), and you have to make amends, change your ways, and be certain you never hurt anyone sexually again. If you stop and look at yourself and your actions, however, you can see that although you have done this and other hurtful things in your life, you have done some good things too. You are a person of real worth. Don't give up on yourself; remember that you can choose to do good things, just as you have sometimes chosen to hurt others.

The next exercise can help you put your offense (and any others) in perspective.

EXERCISE 28. NEGATIVE VS. POSITIVE

On the left side of the chart below, write down all the negative things other people would say about you or you might think about yourself for committing your offense. These words might include such words as "pervert," "crazy person," "weirdo," etc. Then on the right side of the chart, write all the positive words you could use to describe yourself, such as "caring," "smart," "responsible". . . whatever best fits you. Think of all the words you can. Don't be afraid to say good things about yourself. Ask others, if you get stuck and have difficulty thinking of words for either side. You should have at least 10 words on each side.

NEGATIVE DESCRIPTIONS OF ME	POSITIVE DESCRIPTIONS OF ME
1)__________	__________
2)__________	__________
3)__________	__________
4)__________	__________
5)__________	__________
6)__________	__________
7)__________	__________
8)__________	__________
9)__________	__________
10)__________	__________
12)__________	__________
13)__________	__________

Look at these lists. Now think of what percentage of your time you spent doing the things that resulted in the negative descriptions of you and what percentage of your time you spend doing the things listed under positive descriptions. Write the percentage above each column. Realistically, most people spend more than half of their time doing positive things. So, you are mainly a good person. This is important to remember.

What you think of yourself is called *self-esteem.* Your self-esteem can go up or down depending on when and where you are. You gain your self-esteem from a variety of different sources – from your parents, other family members, friends, from what you accomplish in school and in your life. As we mentioned, your self-esteem was probably at an all-time low after you were caught. Studies have also shown that the self-esteem of persons committing sex offenses is often very low both right before they commit the offense and in general.

Building self-esteem is, therefore, a part of learning relapse prevention, as is planning how to protect yourself when you have low self-esteem. Low self-esteem – that is, feeling crummy about yourself – should be a red flag, indicating to you that you are entering a danger zone for reoffending.

Family members, teachers, friends and others give you both verbal and non-verbal messages about your worth as a person. Negative verbal messages include calling you names that make you feel bad about yourself (like "stupid") or telling you negative messages about your behavior (like "You never do anything right"). On the other hand, positive verbal messages can raise your self-esteem. For instance, being called "attractive" is likely to make you feel confident and good looking, and being told "you are such a good student" makes you feel smart.

Non-verbal messages are things that are done or not done that make you feel better or worse about yourself. For example, if your father takes only your brother fishing or for visits, you would probably feel like he didn't care about you, and therefore you must not be worth caring about. On the other hand, if your mother spent time and effort rebuilding and fixing up a car for you, you are likely to feel very valued. If she went to all that trouble just for you, you must be worth a lot.

The following exercise looks at some of the self-esteem messages you got from your family, friends, and people at school, what you think of yourself now, and some ways you can increase your self-esteem.

EXERCISE 29. LOOKING AT SELF-ESTEEM

I) **Family:**

A) What are some of the verbal and nonverbal messages you received from your family about your self-worth?

____

____

B) Who valued you most in your family? ____________________________

How did that person show it? __________________________________

____

____

C) Who did you look up to the most in your family? ______________________________
Why? ______________________________

____

Do you have some of those qualities? ________ Which ones?______________________

____

2) **School:**

A) What messages did you get about your self-worth from most of your teachers? ______________

____

____

B) Was there a teacher who really valued you? ______________________________
What did that teacher do or say that made you feel that way? ______________________

____

C) How did that make you feel? ______________________________

____

3) **Friends:**

A) What are some of the verbal and non-verbal messages you have gotten from your friends about your self-worth? ______________________________

____

____

B) Do you have any friends who really think highly of you? What have they said or done which gives you that impression? ______________________________

____

____

C) Do you have a friend you think highly of? How do you show or tell your friend what you think of him or her? ______________________________

____

____

____

4) **Your Experiences and You:**

A) Write down something that happened in your life that made you feel very good about yourself (like you were a winner, smart, strong, capable, or creative). ______________________

____

____

B) Write down something that happened in your life that made you feel bad about yourself (like inadequate, powerless, worthless, or stupid).______________________________

____

____

C) How are you feeling about yourself right now? ______________________

Why? ______________________

____

D) List four things you have done or could do that would make you feel better about yourself.

1) ______________________
2) ______________________
3) ______________________
4) ______________________

E) Whom do you look up to the most?______________ List four reasons you look up to that person.

1) ______________________
2) ______________________
3) ______________________
4) ______________________

Do you have any of these qualities? ______________________

Which ones? ______________________

____

Would you feel better about yourself if you had these qualities?______________________

____

How do you know when your self-esteem is low? Usually you feel depressed, angry, frustrated, powerless, worthless, unloved, stupid, or any number of other painful emotions we discussed in the last chapter. When you check in on how you are feeling, it is good to see if the emotions are connected to your level of self-esteem. You will usually find that your emotions and your self-worth go hand-in-hand.

There are various ways to increase your self-esteem. The most effective ways are through personal achievement (the result of successful, positive risk taking) and helping others. Personal achievements could be something like trying out for the basketball team and making it. Can you think of some personal achievements or successful positive risks you have taken that increased your self-esteem? Or have you done some things that have helped others and made you feel better about yourself? Try to fit these types of experiences into your life. You will increase your feelings of self-worth if you do.

Your *self-talk* can also increase or decrease your self-esteem. For example, when you feel like you are worthless, if you say to yourself, "Nobody likes me, I'm stupid, I'm ugly, I'm a creep," you will feel much worse about yourself. On the other hand, if you say to yourself, "My best friend likes me, I am good at playing the guitar, I'm a kind person, I did something really nice for my grandmother yesterday," you will think better of yourself. Feeling better can include physical descriptions of yourself, reflections of what others think of you, and positive things you have accomplished.

The next exercise gives you the opportunity to increase the self-esteem of the person described.

EXERCISE 30. BUILDING SELF-ESTEEM

Fill in the blanks with positive statements the person could have said to himself or herself which would increase feelings of self-worth:

1) Marylou's relationship just broke up. She feels like she is worthless and will never have another relationship. What could she say to herself to raise her self-esteem? ______________________________

____

____

2) Todd's step-father called him stupid and worthless. What could Todd say to himself? ______________

____

____

3) Rico just got busted (arrested) for stealing. He feels really worthless. What could he say to himself? ________

____

____

____

4) Bill started a new school, and some of the guys made fun of the way he looks. He feels unpopular and worthless. What could he say to himself? ______________________________

____

____

____

5) Word got out around school that Erin was sexually active with lots of guys. She feels that people view her as a "slut." What could she say to herself? ______________________________

____

____

____

6) Shiro's best friend found out that Shiro is gay and won't talk to him. Shiro feels worthless and different. What could he say to himself? ______________________________

____

____

____

7) Rick's teacher caught him cheating on a test and sent him to the office. Rick feels real crummy about himself. What could he say to himself? ______________________________

____

____

8) Josh's teacher called him a "worthless piece of trash" when he talked back to her in class. ______________

What could he say to himself? ______________________________

____

____

9) After Carol got an A on her biology test, a guy in Carol's class called her a teacher's pet and said she only got the high grade because the teacher had a "thing" for her. Carol knows the teacher likes her. She thinks, "I only got this grade because the teacher likes me. I'm not really that smart." What can she say to herself? ____________________

____

____

____

10) Carl just said something really silly to a girl he likes. He feels like a total fool. What can he say to himself? _

____

____

____

11) Think of how you felt about yourself when you were arrested for your sex offense. What could you have said to yourself to help you regain your self-esteem? ____________________

____

____

____

In all the cases above, bad things either happened or were said that resulted in the persons' thinking badly of themselves. Sometimes nothing bad happens, or even good things happen, but we put ourselves down because of a past history of feeling badly about ourselves. For example, if you got a "C" grade on an algebra test, you could say to yourself, "Most people got better grades than I did." That is putting yourself down, and then you might feel stupid. On the other hand if you said to yourself, "Hallelujah, I passed. This was a really hard test, and I'm proud of myself. Maybe if I study even more, I can get a higher grade," you would feel much better about yourself.

Negative statements that minimize or discount the positive things you've done are put-downs. Thinking positively of what you have done – though without exaggerating – will help improve your self-esteem. These positive statements are referred to as *self-endorsing* statements.

In the following exercise, change the negative self-put-down statements to self-endorsing ones.

EXERCISE 31. SELF-ENDORSING STATEMENTS

1) Johanna won second prize at the all-city art competition. She said to herself, "I didn't win first place so I must be second rate." What self-endorsing statement could Johanna have made to herself instead? ____________________

____

____

2) Steve fixed the carburetor of his friend's car. He said to himself, "Anyone could have fixed it." What could he have said to himself instead? ____________________

____

____

3) Roderigo came from Mexico. He was fluent in English within three months. He said to himself, "I'm not especially smart. Anyone could have learned English in that length of time." What could he have said to himself instead? ________

____

____

4) Mike built a table in woodshop. He said to himself, "It doesn't look professional." What could he have said to himself instead? ____

____

5) Lee hurriedly cleaned his room up. He said to himself, "I don't know why I did this. It will just get messy again." What could he have said to himself instead? ____

____

6) Will was asked to be in charge of the Christmas party at his residential center. He said to himself, "I guess they couldn't find anyone else." What could he have said to himself instead? ____

____

____

7) Think of a time you did something pretty good or were complimented and discounted it. What happened, and what did you say to yourself that put yourself down? ____

What could you have said to yourself instead that would have shown appreciation for yourself? ____________

____

____

Changing your thinking, as you have seen, can improve your self-esteem. But don't forget that *doing* positive things can work even better. If you try hard to achieve some worthwhile goal or go out of your way to go to the aid of someone less fortunate, you will probably like yourself a lot better.

Just how self-esteem fits in with the *Offense Chain* is an important part of the Relapse Prevention puzzle. In case you haven't already guessed it, everything in this book is aimed at keeping you from moving down that *Offense Chain* to another sex offense. Let us look at how it works.

If you feel badly about yourself (have low self-esteem), you are less likely to think of negative outcomes when a *SUD (Seemingly Unimportant Decision)* has to be made. Even if you have molested in the past, for example, with low self-esteem you are less likely to say, "No, I can't," when asked now to babysit. Your fear of saying "no" is because you don't want anyone to think badly of you. You think they will like you better or approve of you more if you say "yes."

Saying "yes" will place you in a *Dangerous Situation.* Because you feel bad about yourself, you are more likely to turn to the child, who looks up to you, for affection and sex. So you *Lapse*, fantasizing or taking that first step toward reoffending. It is easier to *Give Up* at that point, because you already feel you are no good, and think, "Why not go the whole way? I'm already a loser."

In Exercise 32 you will see how improving your self-esteem can help you prevent yourself from committing an offense, and how changing your thoughts or self-talk can affect your self-esteem.

EXERCISE 32. SELF-ESTEEM IN THE OFFENSE CHAIN

Write in what Andy could have said to himself to increase his self-esteem at each step of the way and that would prevent him from moving down the offense chain.

1) Seventeen-year-old Andy long ago molested his little brother. He just moved home after two years of living in a foster home. According to his probation rules, Andy is never at any time to be alone with any children under 16. Andy's mother knows the rules, but her babysitter didn't come in and she needs to go to work. She asks Andy to babysit. He says, "Mom, you know I can't do that." She angrily shouts, "You are a worthless good-for-nothing. You never help me with anything." Because he feels so bad about himself, Andy finally agrees (*SUD*). What could Andy have said to himself to feel better so he wouldn't have needed to agree to babysit? ____________________

____

____

____

____

2) After Andy agreed to babysit, his little brother tells him that he is the best brother in the world. Andy gives him a big hug and cuddles him on his lap (*Dangerous Situation*), because Andy thinks no one else in the world cares about him. What could Andy have said to himself to counteract his feelings of worthlessness and mistaken belief that no one else in the world cared or would care about him? ____________________

____

____

____

____

3) Andy begins to fantasize about molesting his brother (*Lapse*), because he believes he is so worthless that nobody else will ever want to have sex with him. What could Andy say to himself to counteract his negative self-image? ____________________

____

____

____

____

4) Andy unzips his pants and begins to take them off (*Giving Up*). He thinks about stopping and running out of the house, like he had learned in group, but feels so awful about himself that he figures, "I'm already no good and worthless. What's one more offense?" What could he have said to himself about his self-worth that might have prevented him from offending at this point? ____________________

____

____

____

____

You can see from all of the exercises we have done that lots of different thoughts, feelings, and decisions contribute to whether you relapse and reoffend or whether you can succeed in your commitment never to offend again. Knowing yourself, patting yourself on the back when you have done well, not putting yourself down, and improving your self-esteem can all help you to stop at any point in your offense chain before you reoffend.

Now let us review some of the specifics of what you have learned in this chapter on *Understanding Yourself.*

SUMMARY

You can now:

1) Better understand who you are – your physical, mental, emotional, behavioral, and family characteristics, your life and what is important to you, what you want to change, and what your goals are
2) Realize that most of the time you are a positive, worthwhile person
3) Know more about the sources of your self-esteem – family, school. friends, and experiences
4) Know how to check in on your esteem level
5) Know some ways to increase your self-esteem
   a) By personal achievement (or successful, positive risk-taking)
   b) By helping others
   c) Through positive self-talk
6) Understand how self-esteem fits into the *Offense Chain*
7) Recognize how increasing self-esteem through more positive self-talk can prevent reoffense

NOTES

CHAPTER EIGHT

VICTIMS

Everyone is a victim at some time in life. But what exactly is a victim? And how do you know if you have been or are being victimized?

In defining the word "victim," the dictionary includes the following:

1) a person who suffers from a *destructive* or *injurious* action;

2) a person who is deceived or cheated.

As sex offenders, most of you are victims of the types defined by the first two statements, and you have victimized others in the same ways. When you committed your sex offense, you caused your victim to suffer from a destructive or injurious action. You might have denied it or rationalized it away at the time, or you still may not quite believe that your victim suffered great harm from what you did.

There are reasons you didn't pay attention to the fact that you would be victimizing someone when you committed your sex offense. You may have lost touch with how you yourself were victimized, what you felt then, and your own upset, hurt, or confused feelings after you were victimized or molested. For example, if you were sexually molested when you were younger, you may have felt that this was the only time anyone ever showed love to you; then you *rationalized* your own molesting behavior as giving "love" to someone else. If you were physically beaten or are discriminated against because of race or other reasons, you may have felt rage from the violence and unfairness perpetrated against you, and then you acted it out in a sexual way on someone else, not even considering what your victim might feel. Or you may have been sexually molested over and over again at an early age and now feel like you *need* sexual gratification like a video junkie *needs* Nintendo, and it's the only way your body feels good. You might be thinking that since you were so routinely victimized and it didn't seem to bother you, so why should it bother your victim?

In each case, your own victimization might have kept you from understanding and connecting with the negative emotions your victim might feel and the effects he/she might suffer. Otherwise, you probably wouldn't have sexually offended, because you are basically a good person and good people try not to hurt others.

"Abuse" is the term we use to describe the *destructive* or *injurious* actions suffered by victims. We have found that many adolescent sex offenders have also suffered some kind of abuse themselves, usually either sexual abuse, physical abuse, emotional abuse or some combination. Knowing that you've been abused and understanding how it affected you can help you understand your offending behavior and help you not to do it again. But having been a victim is not an excuse for self-pity or destructive behavior, and it is never an excuse for sexual offending.

Because whatever experiences people have had in their lives usually color their view of the world, they may think that such experiences are normal and usual. We often underestimate the severity of the abuses we suffer. The first four histories below are true examples of harmful or injurious acts adolescents experienced, even though they didn't connect these acts with the terms *abuse* or *victimization*. The fifth history deals with another way people handle severe abuse, by *dissociating*, or "going away " in their minds. That is, they lose themselves. They detach themselves from their feelings and sometimes even from conscious awareness in order to get through the abuse. Sometimes they really, honestly have no memory of being abused or, in some cases, even abusing. (This is a little different from what happens when people *deny* their own history of being abused and their abuse of others. People who *deny* know that they were abused and are abusing, but are afraid or ashamed to admit it.)

Read these five histories over carefully. Do any parts of them seem similar to what happened to you or what you did? Even if they do not seem similar, can you see how you lost touch with your feelings about your own abuse? Can you see how your victim might have felt? As you read these histories, remember that not all people who experienced abuse then abuse someone else. Abuse is not an excuse for offending against others. Looking at any victimization you might have experienced gives you *information* about where some of your thoughts and feelings come from. You can then *use* this information to help you understand and change your thoughts, feelings, and behavior and prevent yourself from reoffending.

1) Eric's two older brothers would masturbate in front of him when he was six and they were 14 and 16. They would also mutually masturbate and fondle Eric. Eric wanted to be included by them because he looked up to his big brothers. He felt a little funny when they touched him and made him touch them, but he never said anything to anyone. When Eric was 14, he was arrested for doing similar acts with a 6-year-old neighbor boy. Since Eric didn't think he was abused, he didn't think he abused the neighbor, either.

2) Angela's father was an alcoholic. He would come home drunk and throw things. Pretty often she had to dodge flying lamps, ashtrays, books, and dishes. Often he didn't miss, and one time Angela had to have stitches when she was cut by a glass ashtray her father threw. Angela's father usually didn't remember what he had done, and always apologized anyway the next day. Angela's mother said her father was a good man but suffered from the disease of alcoholism. Angela didn't think she was abused, because several of her friends' fathers did the same thing, and besides, her father didn't know what he was doing. She believed her father loved her. Angela was not sexually abused. When Angela was 13, she painfully yanked and twisted the penis of the 4-year-old boy she was babysitting.

3) Victor's mother had to raise his brothers and him alone, since their father didn't help or come around at all. She had a hard time making ends meet, and would get really frustrated when she felt that the boys were stirring up trouble or not trying hard enough, especially Victor. Victor had trouble in school, because of his learning disorder. He was smart, but he couldn't read or write very well. Because school was so hard for him, he often wouldn't try. His mother got very angry with him when he refused to do his homework and brought home bad reports from school. She yelled at him, "You are stupid. You will never amount to anything. You are just as worthless as your father." Victor thought she was probably right. When he was 16, Victor went to a party and started to make-out in back room with a girl he met there. When she wanted to stop, he didn't listen to her, and forced her to have sex.

4) When Bubba was 10 and his brother Dylan was 16, they lived in a house that was right next door to an older man who lived alone. Bubba and Dylan's bedroom window was right next to one of the windows in the neighbor's house. The neighbor used to stare into Bubba's window and masturbate when Bubba and Dylan were dressing and undressing. Dylan thought it was funny,

and deliberately undressed in front of the window. When Bubba was 14, he was arrested for indecently exposing himself at the elementary school. He said he thought it was a big joke.

5) Daniel's mother and step-father treated him very badly. They chained him under the house. When Daniel wasn't quick enough to obey, his step-father bent him over and forcibly had anal sex with him (anal sex, also called "sodomy" or "sodomizing," is when a male puts his penis in a person's bottom, or anus). They beat him with chains, and killed his pet dog in front of him. When Daniel was being abused, he would kind of black out, and another part of him would kind of take over, a part that didn't feel anything. Daniel was taken away from his home by the state when he was 8. He had no memory of what happened to him, but he was arrested three years later for forcibly sodomizing a 3-year-old boy. Daniel says he vaguely remembers grabbing the child, but nothing more. He has no feelings about either abusing or being abused. He has no idea what his victim might have felt.

(This last history is a very extreme case. While many victims report that they forgot about being abused for a period of several years, it is quite rare not to remember abusing others in the present. People who claim not to remember abusing others usually know what they did. They *deny* their offense to protect themselves because of fear, shame, and guilt.)

All five of these teenagers were abused and abused others. The abuse they suffered caused them emotional or physical pain at the time (even if they closed off the feelings or forgot about the abuse) and was destructive to them. Even though all of them minimized the severity of what happened to them (perhaps because they wanted it not to matter and they wanted to be tough) the abuse caused problems to them later on. The abuse they experienced was *one* of the major reasons they abused others. The abuse left them with feelings of rage, fear, and powerlessness. They acted out their feelings by sexually abusing others. Because they were not aware of how damaging the abuse they had suffered was to them, they didn't understand the hurt they caused their victims.

Let us look at each of these histories a little more closely. In the first case, Eric was much too young to be engaging in sex with others, and although he believed he had consented, he was really coerced. *Coerced* means that the person who convinced him was in a position of power over him, much older, much stronger, etc. Eric wanted approval by his brothers and wanted to be included in their closeness. If his brothers had not been abusive, he could have gotten this approval in a healthy way rather than by participating in a sexual act. Eric pushed down his own negative feelings about what was happening, so that now all he can remember is feeling "a little funny." Because Eric can't remember his own feelings, he did not understand that his victim might feel frightened, sickened, or powerless in the situation. He doesn't even realize that the neighbor boy might have agreed to participate because the boy wanted the same kind of approval and caring from Eric that Eric wanted from his brothers.

In the second scenario, Angela was probably terrified for her own safety and furious at what her father was putting her through. But she could never recognize and express her anger, because her father kept apologizing and her mother kept making excuses for her father's behavior. So the anger built up, and when Angela was a teenager she took it out indirectly on a 4-year-old boy. Because Angela's fear and anger were never acknowledged, she didn't appreciate how terrified and afraid the little boy might be. Angela didn't even have any idea why she did it

In the third history, Victor was put down again and again because of his learning disorder. He was frustrated with school, angry at his mother, and furious with himself. He felt that nobody loved, understood or would help him. He used sex for the missing love and understanding, and acted out his anger in the date rape. He was so filled with anger and emptiness that he couldn't connect with what his victim might feel. Since nobody cared about him, he cared neither about himself or others.

In the fourth history, Bubba was exposed to sex at too young an age and in an inappropriate way. Because his brother had given the neighbor's acts such attention, and because Bubba was out of touch with his own needs for attention and excitement, when he was 14 he acted out his feelings in the same way as the neighbor had. Since Dylan thought of his neighbor's actions as funny, Bubba forgot how uncomfortable he felt watching his neighbor masturbate, and only thought of the excitement of doing it. He didn't think that the children at the school might have been afraid of him, since he hadn't been afraid of the neighbor. He forgot his discomfort and rationalized that it was funny because his brother had said it was.

In the final history, Daniel was the subject of such severe abuse that he literally shut down his emotions and his consciousness. At times his rage at what happened to him would take over later on when he was in a safer situation. He wasn't even aware of what he was feeling. Sometimes he wasn't even aware of what he was doing. His separation from his own feelings when he was abused prevented him from recognizing or caring about what his victim might feel. Because he is the most out of touch with what happened to him and what he did, he is the most at risk of repeating his sexually offending behavior.

Exercise 33 gives you the opportunity to examine your own abuse.

EXERCISE 33. LOOKING AT MY OWN ABUSE

Write "yes" on the blank line next to the items that apply to you. Think about how often they happened. Were they everyday or rare occurrences?

I) **Physical Abuse**:

a) How were you punished or treated when you were a child? Were you or have you ever been:

Hit with a belt ______________ Hit with kitchen utensils_______ Hit with a stick______________

Hit with a coat hanger _______ Struck with closed fists _______ Hit by thrown objects ________

Kicked ____________________ Painfully pinched ___________ Painfully tickled______________

Burned____________________ Cut _______________________ Drugged ___________________

Thrown across the room or against a wall _____________________ Choked____________________

Head held underwater (sink, toilet, pool, stream) _____ Tied or chained up ______________________

Forced to stay out in the cold ________________ Starved (not just missed a meal) ____________

Had your head hit against the wall or floor ________ Had your hair pulled out _________________

Had food forcibly stuffed down your throat_________ Beaten with cords or whips ______________

Made to stand in a painful or uncomfortable position for a long period of time____________________

Other ____

All of these types of punishment are abusive. If they, or any similar abusive physical acts were perpetrated against you, you are a victim of physical abuse.

b) Who did this to you? ______

c) If you were a victim of physical abuse, how did you feel during the time you were being abused?

Angry ______ Afraid ______ Sad ______
Bad ______ I deserved it ______ Picked on ______
Worthless ______ Unloved ______ Unwanted ______
Powerless ______ Strong enough to take it ______ No feelings at all ______
Other ______

______

d) How did you feel right after the abuse?

Angry ______ Afraid ______ Sad ______
Bad ______ Picked on ______ Worthless ______
Unloved ______ Unwanted ______ Nervous ______
Like getting even ______ Like "you can't get to me" ______ Frustrated ______
Wanting to run away ______ Obedient ______ More disobedient ______
Other ______

______

e) As a result of your physical abuse, do you:

Fight a lot? ______ Have a quick, hot temper? ______
Often hit your brothers or sisters? ______ Punch walls? ______
Throw objects? ______ Kick things? ______
Get even with people who cross you? ______ Not get close to anyone? ______
Think most people are out to get you? ______ Hate most people? ______
Feel like you deserved the abuse? ______ Not care? ______
Want to beat up your perpetrator? ______ Act bad? ______
Do you do other negative behaviors possibly as a result of your abuse? ______

______

______

2) **Sexual Abuse:**

a) Violent sex: Did anyone ever use force or threats to:

Rape you (intercourse) ______ Sodomize you (anal sex) ______
Feel you up (fondling) ______ Make you perform oral sex ______
Perform oral sex on you ______ Masturbate you ______
Make you look at his/her sexual parts ______ Make you masturbate him/her ______
Grab any of your sexual parts ______ Insert objects inside you ______
Take sexual photographs of you ______ Make you watch any sexual acts ______
Make you participate in any pornographic films ______
Make you have sex with others for money or gifts (prostitution) ______

Make you have sex with animals ______________________________

Make you perform group sex acts______________________________

Make you do anything sexual with yourself. What?______________________________

____

Other ______________________________

____

Who did this to you?______________________________

What force or threat of force did they use?______________________________

____

Were you sexually aroused? (This is a normal reaction.)______________________________

Do you feel sexual feelings now when you think about being sexually abused?______________________________

____

b) Coercive sex: Did anyone with more power or status convince, bribe, or trick you to do or submit to any of the following acts?

Sexual intercourse______________

Masturbate him/her______________

Feel you up (fondling) ______________

Put his penis between your legs ______________

Make you have oral sex him/her ______________

Rub up against you______________

Perform group sex acts______________

Tickle your sexual areas ______________

Take sexual photos of you ______________

Have sex with animals ______________

Make you undress and spank you ______________

Anal sex (sodomy) ______________

Masturbate him/herself in front of you ______________

Let him/her masturbate you ______________

Put his/her mouth on your sexual parts ______________

Pretend to touch your sexual parts for a medical reason _

Prostitute yourself ______________

Perform sex for others______________

Teach you about sex by showing you how to do it ____

Show you pornographic books or movies ______________

Put any objects into your anus or vagina______________

Make you undress and humiliate you ______________

Other ______________________________

____

Who did this to you?______________________________

How did that person get you to go along? ______________________________

____

____

____

Did you feel sexually aroused during the acts? (This is a normal reaction.)

____

Did you feel close or loved? ______________________________

Did you miss the sexuality when it stopped? (This is also a normal reaction.) ______________________________

Do you feel sexual feelings now when you think about being sexually coerced? ______________________________

c) *Attempted* sexual acts: Did anyone ever *try* to do any of the above to you or with you? (This is sexual abuse too.)

_______________ Which acts? _______________

d) Did you ever go along with being sexual with someone when you really wanted to say "No" or "Stop"? ______

When? _______________

With whom? _______________

Why? _______________

e) How did you feel when the sexual abuse above was happening? (You may have many or mixed feelings, good and bad.)

Afraid ______	Uncomfortable ______	Embarrassed ______
In shock ______	Not there(dissociated) ______	Special ______
Weird ______	Helpless ______	Terrified ______
Disgusted ______	Confused ______	Loved ______
No good ______	Deserving of it ______	Picked on ______
Scarred for life ______	Dirty ______	Unloved ______
Special ______	Chosen ______	Sexy ______
Aroused ______	Attractive ______	Furious ______
Guilty ______	Guilty but aroused ______	Ashamed ______
Important ______	Different from others ______	Mature ______
Powerful ______	Other ______	

f) How do you feel about it now?

Angry ______	Still afraid ______	Sad ______
Bad ______	Used ______	Worthless ______
Scarred ______	Like it was no big deal ______	Guilty ______
Humiliated ______	Embarrassed ______	Unloved ______
Special ______	Lonely ______	Powerless ______
Mature ______	Different from others ______	Smarter than others ______
Disgusted ______	Sexier ______	Cheap ______
Like getting even ______	Dirty ______	Different ______
Stupid ______	Often depressed ______	Deserving of it ______
Confused ______	Ripped off of some of my childhood ______	

Other _______________

_______________ Nothing _______________

g) How may the sexual abuse have affected you? Do you:

Stay alone a lot ______	Need to be with people ______	Drink a lot ______
Use drugs ______	Have a hot temper ______	Fight a lot ______
Run away from home ______	Have trouble concentrating ______	Daydream a lot ______
Hold feelings in ______	Go along with anything (not say no) ______	
Avoid sex ______	Think about sex all the time ______	

Have sex more often than classmates ________ Have less sex than classmates ________
Use sex to get things ________ Constantly masturbate ________
Use pornography ________ Put yourself down ________ Cut school a lot ________
Have to be perfect ________ Not trust others ________ Use food to avoid feelings ________
Get even ________ Act tough ________ Break rules ________
Break the law ________ Not care about the future ________ Hurt others ________
Think about suicide ________ Try to commit suicide ________
Destroy things (of others or your own?) ________ Run with a gang ________
Other ________ No effect ________

3) **Emotional Abuse:** Write down names you were called and things that were said or done to you that have made you see yourself in a negative light. While everyone has been put down in some ways, if these things happened on a regular basis, they can be considered emotional abuse. You will have the opportunity to decide afterward if they reached the level of emotional abuse.

NAMES CALLED ("stupid," "slut," racial slurs, or social put-downs)	**THINGS SAID** ("you'll never amount to anything")	**NONVERBAL MESSAGES** (always doing things for your brother and never for you)
BY FATHER: ________	________	________
________	________	________
________	________	________
________	________	________
________	________	________
BY MOTHER: ________	________	________
________	________	________
________	________	________
________	________	________
________	________	________
BY A STEP-PARENT: ________	________	________
________	________	________
________	________	________
________	________	________
________	________	________
BY OTHER FAMILY MEMBERS: ________	________	________
________	________	________
________	________	________
________	________	________

BY A TEACHER: ______________ ______________ ______________

______________ ______________ ______________

______________ ______________ ______________

______________ ______________ ______________

BY OTHER KIDS: ______________ ______________ ______________

______________ ______________ ______________

______________ ______________ ______________

______________ ______________ ______________

a) How often were you given these negative messages? ______________

Talk about this with your friends and group members. Then think about this carefully. Do you think that you were called names, put down more, or given more negative non-verbal or subtle messages a lot of the time? Then decide – have you been emotionally abused?

Constantly? ______________ Often? ______________ Some of the time? ______________

b) How do you think the put-downs you have experienced have affected your life (even if they didn't reach the level of emotional abuse)? Do you think you may:

Have lower self-esteem ______ Have fewer goals ______ Have less friends ______

Be more depressed ______ Feel more frustrated ______ Not try ______

Use alcohol more ______ Use other drugs more ______ Feel angrier ______

Feel stupid ______ Feel helpless ______ Feel resentful ______

Try harder ______ Feel like a loser ______ Rebel more ______

Care less about what happens to you ______ Care less about others ______

Care less about everything ______ Get along worse with family ______

Want to get one over on everyone ______ Do criminal acts ______

Other ______________

____

____

____

____

Read this exercise over once a week or once a month. It is good to put the past behind you, but you need to process (or work through) the feelings you felt during and after the abuse you experienced. When you have processed and resolved these feelings, they are less likely to influence what you think, feel, and do, particularly about sexually offending. "Processing" your experiences simply means getting in touch with your feelings and thoughts at the time of your abuse and putting them in the proper perspective. If you were victimized (abused), you may be blaming yourself instead of the perpetrator, such as thinking of yourself as stupid to have let it go on. Or you may be acting out some of the rage you feel, instead of working through it in a healthy way.

If you have been abused either physically, sexually, or emotionally and you have no feelings or feel it was no big deal, you are probably out of touch with your feelings and need more work to zone in on them. You are much more likely to commit another sex offense or another hurtful act if you are unaware of your anger, frustration, lack of self-esteem, or other feelings left over from the abuse you received. If you don't understand your feelings, you will not see the signs leading to reoffense. Unless you notice them, you cannot change your thoughts, feelings, and behaviors to avoid or escape dangerous situations and lapse points.

Some of you were not abused. Not everyone who sexually abuses others experienced abuse as a child. As you talk to other friends, you will find that some experienced terrible sexual or physical or emotional abuse but never acted out in a hurtful way, and they seem to be pretty well adjusted. On the other hand, many people who were not seriously abused committed sex offenses or other criminal acts. Everyone reacts differently to life experiences, and no two people experience exactly the same thing. Not all people who are abused become abusers and not all people who weren't abused refrain from committing sex offenses or other destructive behaviors.

There probably were some hurtful experiences you had that influenced your decision to offend. People who are basically well adjusted, have good self-esteem, communicate well, relate well to others, and are in touch with feelings usually don't commit sex offenses. Some of the adolescent offenders we've worked with have experienced situations that are hurtful or border on abuse and that created frustration, anger, feelings of abandonment, low self-esteem, a sense of loss, etc. These include such things as:

a) Having a totally dominating father or mother who doesn't listen and makes all the decisions

b) Being left out, used, or not appreciated while living with a parent and step-parent who have kids of their own (half-brothers or -sisters or step-brothers or -sisters)

c) Not having a mother or father, or having a mother or father who never come around

d) Having to live with other relatives or in a foster or adoptive home because parent(s) cannot raise them

e) Having one or both parents who are never available emotionally or aren't there when needed

f) Having a learning disability so school is harder and special classes are necessary

g) Having a speech or other type of impairment or disability

h) Being a different race or religion than most of the kids in school or the neighborhood

i) Having a close friend move away or having a neighbor, classmate, friend, or pet die

These are a few reasons some people have problems that may result in behavior that either hurts others, themselves, or both. Can you think of some other situations that apply in your case?

In the next exercise, you have the opportunity to write down all of the smaller things that bother you, that you wish were different. Don't be afraid of sounding stupid. This is just for you. It is a healthy way of letting it all out.

EXERCISE 34. AIRING GRIPES

1) In the first part of this exercise, just write down as many gripes as you can think of as fast as you can for 10 minutes. Gripes can be anything that is unfair, that you don't like, that is frustrating, irritating, or makes you feel crummy. They can be related to people, events, or just things that happen or are there. Do this as fast as you can. Don't elaborate. Use extra paper if necessary.

2) In this section, look back at the exercise on abuse as well as at the first part of this exercise and pick out the various people who either abused or in some way caused you problems. Who were they? List them below:

Now write a *short* note (just one sentence) to each telling them how you felt when they did what they did and why. For example, "Dad, I always feel worthless and like you think I'm stupid because you never let me decide things for myself," or "Big brother, I felt so uncomfortable, powerless, and stupid when you did those sexual things to me."

TO	HOW YOU FELT	WHEN THAT PERSON DID WHAT ACT?

Look over your list of gripes and the people involved.

Can you discuss the abuses and gripes directly with the person who caused them? Often people are afraid to, afraid of what that person will think of them, afraid of being abused again (or worse), or afraid the other person has forgotten. If you *can* sit down and talk these issues over, you will usually feel better. In some cases, however, the other person is not capable of listening. That is their problem. They are stuck in negative or hurtful behaviors. If the person is not available, won't listen, or is too dangerous to approach, talk some of these things over with someone else, another family member, a friend, or a counselor. It is good to get them out.

You may also want to write a longer letter to someone who has hurt you in some way. You don't have to give it to them. Just the exercise of writing the letter can help you get the feelings out. Every time you get them out in a positive, healthy way, you will feel better. The letter below was written by a 13-year-old girl to her father who molested her. It could just as easily have been written by a boy. Molestation has just as strong an impact on both boys and girls.

Dear Dad,

I am writing to you, because I want you to know what you put me through by molesting me. My life got shattered into tiny bits – a whole lifetime ruined – my whole self destroyed.

Being molested means having feelings that I won't be able to stand having sex with my husband or just not being able to love or touch my husband without it bringing back horrible memories. It means always being scared about getting molested again. It means being prejudiced or holding a grudge against the molester and everyone else who has molested. It means not ever wanting to see the molester again. It means having lots of mixed-up feelings, like being angry, sad, scared and hateful all at the same time. It means crying at night while thinking, "Why? Why did this happen to me?"

Molestation is a very scary thing, and I don't think I can ever forgive you for putting me through HELL by molesting me.

Have you ever had any feelings like this? Has anyone ever done anything hurtful to you that you will never forget? Think hard. If you thought of something, did you list it in Exercise 33? If not, go back and add these things in.

This letter was written by a real girl who sent it to her father. He was in therapy at the time, so he was able to hear and understand what his daughter was feeling. They eventually were able to talk through the issues. The father apologized, took responsibility for what he did, and promised never to hurt her again. After a lot of work in therapy, he asked for – and got – her forgiveness, but she still will never forget what he did and will never fully trust him again.

Often people who write to those who have hurt them, and send the letters, don't get a reply. Remember three things as you work on the exercise below: 1) you are writing this letter to express your feelings; 2) you don't have to send it or, if you do send it, you don't need to get a reply for it to help; 3) this letter is for *you*, a way to help yourself feel better, not for the other person.

Now is the time for you to write your longer letter to someone who hurt you. You can write it to the perpetrator if you were abused, or to a parent, other family member, or friend who has let you down or treated you badly, or even to God.

EXERCISE 35: LETTER TO SOMEONE WHO HURT ME

This letter may be as long or short as you want, but make sure to cover the following topics. (You may want to write more than one letter or a longer letter than there is space for here. Don't hesitate to use extra paper for this.)

1) What you are angry or hurt about or what bothers you (what that person did)

2) What emotions you feel as a result of the abuse or other situation

3) What you think about the person who caused the problem

4) How the abuse or other situation has affected how you act or have behaved

5) What you would like your abuser (or whoever hurt you in some way) to say or do, such as apologize, tell you why he did what he did, say something that shows he or she understands what you have gone through, etc.

Dear ______________________________,

____

____

____

____

____

____

____

____

____

____

____

____

Signed:

Now think over what you wrote. How do you feel about the person who hurt you? Will you forget about the hurt? Will you trust your abuser again? How has (have) your experience(s) affected your outlook on the world? How have your choices been affected by your experience(s)? Really think about this for a while. When you are victimized you are forever changed by your experience. All experiences in life change us. Whether we forgive the person(s) who hurt us or not, we will never quite be the same.

Some people can't seem to write their thoughts and feelings down very well or have trouble putting them in words. If you are one of those people, you may want to draw pictures of what happened to you, what you felt about it, what the perpetrator looks like to you, and how you feel towards the perpetrator.

Other adolescent offenders we have worked with have preferred to put these thoughts and feelings down in a song or poem. This is another good way to express them. One young person even constructed a horror house (like a dollhouse) that showed what happened to him and how he felt.

If someone committed an offense against you, it changed you. It was one of many factors that may have distorted your thinking, made you feel needy or bad about yourself, and contributed to your choice to commit your offense(s). But *you are still responsible for your choices*. You can learn from your hurtful experiences and destructive acts, depending on what you do with them. That is what this book is all about. That is what *Relapse Prevention* means. You can use your past experiences as learning tools to make positive and thoughtful choices and to help you to never repeat your offenses.

Getting in touch with the feelings behind your own victimizations and other painful experiences and situations is an important step toward change. If you know what you are feeling, you will be able to understand better what other people are feeling, so you can avoid hurting them. That is what the next chapter is all about.

SUMMARY

You could have gained the following information from this chapter:

1) A better understanding of definitions of victimization and abuse and what actions they include
2) More about the abuse you may have suffered
3) Awareness of other acts, happenings, or situations that have bothered you
4) Increased awareness of the impact and effects of the abuse and the other situations you experienced upon your feelings, thoughts, and actions
5) Increased awareness of your own emotions
6) Some ways of dealing with what you feel about the people who hurt you and what they did, like writing your thoughts and feelings down – for yourself, in letters, in songs, or in poetry, expressing yourself in artwork, or talking to the person directly
7) Increased awareness of how your life experiences affect your actions
8) Increased understanding that change and the power to make good choices is in your hands

CHAPTER NINE

EMPATHY

Empathy is one of the most important feelings you can learn, and the one most often forgotten by sex offenders when they commit their offenses. Empathy means trying to understand what another person is likely to be thinking and feeling in a given situation. It means trying to put yourself into their shoes.

No two people react to things in the same way. For example, Albert, a 12-year-old boy, felt confused, embarrassed and ashamed when his aunt molested him, while Joe, another 12-year-old who was also molested by an aunt, felt helpless, violated and terrified. Both had painful feelings, but their feelings differed in type and degree. The way the molestations happened, the personalities and past experiences of each of the boys, the relationship each had before with his particular aunt, and many other factors determined their individual responses.

Another example is that of two women who received a series of obscene phone calls. Dana was disgusted and frightened (frightened because she didn't know if the caller knew her address and might come and hurt her), but she was able to function normally afterward. Linda received a similar series of calls. Not only did she feel similar disgust and fright, but she felt so panicky, terrorized, and unsafe that she couldn't eat, sleep, or leave the house for months afterward. Linda's more extreme reaction was due in large part to the fact that she had recently been violently raped. Her terrible feelings from that rape were added to the painful feelings she would have had from the phone calls alone to create a much more devastating response. You can never know what the past experiences of your victim may have been, but it is important to be aware that a chain reaction can be set off by your harmful actions.

An opposite situation is that of Tony and Chuck, two teenagers. Tony came from a tough, gang-ruled neighborhood. Chuck came from a small, safe town. When Tony was robbed by two other teenagers swinging a bat, it was not the first time. While he felt fearful, powerless and angry at the time, he took the robbery in stride. He had learned to turn off a lot of his terror, because he had to do so to survive in his neighborhood. When Chuck was robbed in the same way, it was the first time. He felt terrified and powerless and was emotionally upset for a long time. While both boys experienced fear, helplessness, and violation, Chuck's feelings were much more intense, because he hadn't lived through other experiences of the same type before and feared more for his life. The important thing to recognize, however, is that both boys felt substantially the same emotions, one more intensely than the other due to past experiences.

We cannot actually climb inside the heads of other people to know what they are thinking or feeling, but we can ask, and we can think about what we would have felt in a similar situation. Since you are basically a good person who doesn't want to intentionally hurt innocent people, it is important that you develop *empathy*. Awareness of what victims and others might be feeling can help keep you from reoffending, especially if you did not set out to intentionally hurt someone. You may have been either unaware of what the victim might feel, used distorted thinking to misread what the victim was feeling, or shut off all feelings.

The following exercise can help you tune into the feelings of others.

EXERCISE 36. THINKING ABOUT WHAT OTHERS ARE FEELING

After each of the following situations, list at least three emotions the person might have felt. You can use the feeling words list in Chapter Four to help you.

1) Adam's father came home from work and started picking on Adam. He told Adam he was a lazy, stupid son-of-a-bitch, couldn't do anything right, and that he wished Adam had never been born. How did Adam feel after his father said this?

____

____

____

2) Charlie's girlfriend told him he was the greatest guy in the world – smart, handsome, sexy, and generous. How did Charlie feel when she said this? ______________________________

____

____

3) John worked hard on his English paper. He got an A on it. How did he feel? ____________________

____

____

4) Mary's grandmother always hugged her and baked cookies for her. How did this make Mary feel? ____________

____

____

5) Dennis' parents were alcoholics. They got loud and obnoxious in the evenings when they were drinking. How did Dennis feel when his friends came over to visit? ______________________________

____

____

6) Roger's Dad is in prison. How does Roger feel when everyone is talking about their fathers? ______________

____

____

7) Amy's family is on welfare, and most of her clothes are hand-me-downs. How does she feel when her friends talk about their new clothes and gifts and expensive activities?______________________________

____

____

8) Andy's family is wealthier than any of his friends' families, and he gets to go on much more expensive and faraway vacations than they do. How does he feel when he comes back from an expensive Christmas trip and everyone is telling what they did during the vacation?____

____

____

9) Vikrim is the only East Indian student in the school. How does he feel? __________________________

____

____

10) Walter calls Malcolm a "dirty nigger." How does Malcolm feel? ____________________

____

11) Gina overhears some other girls making fun of how she talks. How does she feel? ____________________

____

12) Some of his so-called friends give Don a hard time because he is white, but he is going with a girl who is African-American. How does he feel? ____________________

____

13) How does Don's girlfriend feel when she finds out that Don's friends are giving him a hard time for going out with her?

____

____

14) Carlos finds a note in his locker that says, "Go back to Mexico, you greaser." How does he feel? ____________________

____

____

15) Peter's brother is gay. How does he feel when his friends make fun of gays? ____________________

____

16) Jason's older brothers got into all kinds of trouble in school and with the law. When his teachers pick on him because he is a member of that family, how does he feel? ____________________

____

17) Because Roland is very artistic, loves to dance, and plays the violin, lots of people think he is gay even though he is not. How does he feel when he hears them saying he is gay? ____________________

____

18) Bart is an outstanding athlete. He is captain of the football team and is outstanding in several different sports. He is gay, but hasn't told anyone. How do you think he feels when he hears the other guys put down gays? ____________________

____

____

19) Aileen has AIDS and knows she will probably die soon. How does she feel when she is with her friends at school?

____

____

20) Darlene is big breasted. All the guys whistle at her as she walks by. How does this make her feel? ____________________

____

____

Based on information given to us by both male and female sexual abuse victims, we can identify certain general feelings that most victims of sexual abuse feel. Sex offenders usually aren't aware of or don't care what their victims are feeling, or make a lot of thinking errors about what their victims feel. Let us see how aware you are of what the victims in the following situations might feel in the next exercise. If you can't seem to figure these out, pretend you are in a similar situation. Then think about how you might feel. It is important for you to be able to do this. If you can't, you probably need to go back and spend more time on Chapters Four and Six.

EXERCISE 37. VICTIM EMPATHY

In this exercise, answer the questions at the end of each situation. Try to give more than one response to each question. Think your answers over carefully.

1) Naomi was grabbed by a stranger at night as she was walking home. He raped her at knifepoint, then let her go. List several emotions she might have felt. ______

______

What might she have felt if she was raped by her brother's friend on the way home from school? ______

______

2) Ricardo was babysitting for Domi, a 7-year-old neighbor boy. He told Domi to pull down his pants. Ricardo then fondled Domi's penis. Afterward, Ricardo told Domi that they would both get into trouble if the boy told anyone. How do you think Domi felt about what Ricardo did to him? ______

How did Domi feel about himself? ______

______

3) Joey exposed his penis and masturbated in front of a woman who was walking through a park at night. How do you think the woman felt? ______

______

How might she have felt if the same thing happened in a crowded department store during the daytime? ______

______

______

4) Allen went into a strange yard and peered in the bathroom window at a woman just as she got out of the shower. She saw him. How do you think she felt? ______

______

5) Dr. Stanford, a skin doctor (dermatologist), told 16-year-old Hillary that he needed to examine her vagina, even though she was there for a rash she had on her arms. She undressed as she was told to. He came in to examine her and rubbed her vaginal area with his hands and penis. How do you think Hillary felt? ______

______

6) Arthur, age 17, was doing photographic studies of children. He told Tanya, an 8-year-old, to take her top off for one photo session, then her pants for another. He photographed her vagina. Why do you think she didn't object? What was she thinking and feeling? ______

______

______

7) Dan went out with Carol. They parked and started to make love. She willingly fondled his penis. But when he pushed her head down to have oral sex, she said no and pulled away. He pushed her head down forcibly and made her suck his penis. How do you think she felt afterward? ______

______

8) Tom told his 11-year-old sister he loved her. He French kissed her and fondled her breasts. She loved him and wanted him to love her, so she did not object. How did she feel afterward? ______

______

9) Carol fondled and stuck her finger in the vagina of her 2-year-old sister as she was diapering her. It hurt the child, who had always loved Carol. What did the child feel afterward? ______________________________

____

10) Hank told his 6-year-old brother Ike to play penises with him. He showed Ike how to masturbate both of them, and told Ike not to tell anyone what they were doing. How did Ike feel the following year when the Child Abuse Prevention Program at school told the children that touching penises was wrong? ______________________________

____

11) Michelle is 14. Her stepfather got into her bed and touched her breasts and vaginal area one night when he was drunk. How did she feel at the time? ______________________________

____

How did she feel the next day when her father was sober? ______________________________

____

How did she feel when she told her mother and her mother told her she was a liar? ______________________________

____

12) Alice had a reputation for being a "party girl." Ronald invited her to a party with five of his male friends. They all sat around and got loaded on booze and pot. Then the boys took Alice's clothes off over her objections and all had sex with her. How did Alice feel at the time? ______________________________

____

Did she feel any differently afterward? If so, how? ______________________________

____

Do you think she would have felt any differently if she had a reputation for being a "good girl?" ______________________________

____

13) Annie was at a party. She got drunk and passed out. She awoke, finding a guy she didn't know on top of her having intercourse with her. How did she feel at the time of awakening? ______________________________

____

If she yelled stop and he didn't? ______________________________

If he put his hand over her mouth and threatened her? ______________________________

____

14) Miguel is 8 years old. His 13-year-old brother and his brother's 14-year-old friend showed him pornographic pictures, masturbated in front of him, and then dry humped him from behind. How do you think Miguel felt at the time? ___

____

When he was 14 years old? ______________________________

____

15) Benny, age 12, made 6-year-old Joshua take his pants down in front of all the children at on the school grounds. Everyone laughed. How did Joshua feel? ______________________________

____

16) Donna, a 13-year-old, put her hand down the front of her 11-year-old school-mate Raymond's pants on the school grounds, and said, "Oh, what a teenie wienie you've got there." Everyone laughed. How did Raymond feel? ______

____

How would he have felt if they were alone on the grounds and she was a stranger?____________________

____

17) Gina, age 14, sometimes wore low-cut dresses to school. Richie and Hugh thought it would be fun to squeeze her breasts. Richie went up to her and did it first. Hugh followed. How do you think Gina felt? ____________________

____

18) Larry was all alone at home one night when he received an obscene phone call. How do you think he felt?

____

Do you think he might have felt differently if his parents were home? If so, how? ____________________

____

19) Nick and his friends think Penny is unfriendly. They decide to "moon" her every time they see her. How does she feel when they expose themselves to her? ____

____

Do you think she feels any differently when she is with her friends and they do it or when she is all alone and they do it? If so, how?____

____

20) Now briefly describe your offense. What did you do and to whom?

How old was your victim? ____

Who was your victim? (relation, friend, acquaintance, stranger?) ____________________

Where was the offense committed? ____________________________________

Who else was there at the time? _____________________________________

What do you think your victim might have felt at the time?__________________________

____

Now? ____

____

If you had difficulty with Exercise 37 or item 20 in the exercise, it may be because you have incorrect information and have formed *Thinking Errors* about how victims feel. People who sexually offend usually use *Thinking Errors* to try to excuse their hurtful behavior so they won't feel so bad about what they did. The next exercise may help you see your own *Thinking Errors* and correct them.

EXERCISE 38. THINKING ERRORS ABOUT VICTIMS

Below is a list of *thinking errors* or *distortions* about what victims feel. As you read over the list, circle the numbers of the thoughts you had about your victim(s). (Leave the spaces beside the thinking errors blank for now.)

1) She/he wanted it. ______________________________

____

2) She/he liked it. ______________________________

____

3) She/he would have said no if he/she didn't want or like it. ______________________________

____

4) If the victim didn't say no, it's okay to do. ______________________________

____

5) It didn't hurt him/her. ______________________________

____

6) It was okay because I did it gently. ______________________________

____

7) It was just a joke. Can't he/she take a joke? ______________________________

____

8) We were just playing around. It didn't mean anything. ______________________________

____

9) She/he was a slut/prick and deserved it. ______________________________

____

10) She/he put out for everyone else, so what's the difference? ______________________________

____

11) It was okay because I care a lot about him/her. ______________________________

____

Read the Corrected Thinking section below. Then go back and write in the corrected thinking that applies to each of the statements above in the spaces following them. Pay particular attention to the items that you circled.

Corrected Thinking: Victims do not want to be victimized. They may not *show* that they don't like the abuse because they are afraid or ashamed. People who are drunk or who have been sexually active with others do not want or deserve sexual abuse. People should have control of their own bodies. Nobody has a right to do anything to anyone who doesn't want it. Nobody has a right to invade the body privacy of another person without consent, no matter how sexually active the person has been in the past, or even if the person has been a prostitute.

Often victims have a hard time saying no. No one listened to them when they said "no" in the past, or they are afraid of being physically hurt or emotionally rejected by saying no. *It is your responsibility to ask and be tuned-in to what your potential same-age sexual partner wants.* "Tuning-in" means being aware of body language as well as words. (You'll learn more about body language later in this book.)

Just because a sexual act is done gently or the victim is not physically hurt does not mean the victim has not been hurt emotionally. The victim still feels violated, helpless, ashamed, damaged, afraid, and a lot of other painful emotions, and may feel this way for a long time, even forever.

Young children, in particular, don't know enough yet to make good decisions about sex. They are not ready to understand the consequences of what they do, and whether they will be hurt or not. The same is true for victims who have mental problems, are developmentally disabled (mentally retarded), or are drunk or drugged. Even though child or impaired victims may say they liked the sexual conduct (either to save face or because they liked the attention), they are very hurt or damaged by sexual activity they are not ready for or that is not right for them at that age. Once again, *it is your responsibility,* as someone who is older and who knows more, *not to do anything to a child or impaired person that might damage him/her.*

Abused children usually feel betrayed, angry, used, dirty, scarred for life, different from other children, disgusted by sex, or may wrongly use sex to gain power rather than pleasure as they get older. They also may act out sexually at too early an age, and, in addition to the emotional harm, may be physically injured if penetrated.

Many offenders think their behavior was a joke or just playing around, but they have hurt their victims. It is not a joke to most victims. The victims are usually confused, embarrassed, humiliated, and feel powerless during these so-called "jokes" and "playing around." When these offenders look more closely at their behavior, they usually discover that they were feeling bad, down, annoyed, angry, or bored when they offended. They used their hostile behavior to make themselves feel better by making their victim(s) feel bad.

Common emotions felt by victims who know their perpetrators are embarrassment, confusion, anger, fright, disgust, violation of their person, and betrayal. Victims who are strangers to the perpetrator, such as victims of exposers or phone callers, are also often terrified of what this scary person *might* do. Will the offender grab them, take them away, or kill them? And when some strange man sticks out his penis and masturbates in public, the victim is not "turned on," but usually feels helpless and scared, even if the victim tries not to show it.

Victims of rape are particularly terrified for their lives. This terror may continue for years, even when the offender has been caught. Because of what happened to them, victims feel that life is not safe anywhere. They may also have nightmares, flashbacks, cold sweats, and a variety of emotional and physical problems.

If you have any questions about what the victim of your particular crime(s) might have felt, talk to your counselor. Your counselor has probably talked to many victims of the kind of offense you committed and can give you further insight into what they might have felt.

The next exercise continues to raise your awareness of what sexual abuse victims feel. But instead of writing, you can play out the different scenarios, two people for each, in front of the group.

EXERCISE 39. EMPATHY ROLE PLAYS

In your treatment group play out the following situations with a partner. Decide between the two of you who will play which character. Make up your own lines as you go along. Say what you think your character would be saying at that time. After each scenario, have the group tell what the characters seemed to be feeling.

1) A police officer questions 5-year-old Jimmy about how his brother molested him. Show how the officer might treat the little child. Act out how the 5-year-old feels during the interview and about what his brother did to him.

2) Dora tells her mother that her older brother is molesting her. Have her mother at first think that Dora is lying just to get the brother in trouble. Then finally have Dora convince her mother that it is true. Think about why a mother would first disbelieve her daughter and then be convinced. Think about how Dora feels when her mother disbelieves her, and then how she feels once her mother believes her, as well as how she feels about the molestation in general. Share this with the group.

Role play the same situation again, except now *Dan* is trying to convince his mother that his brother is molesting him. How might it be different for Dan than for Dora? Is the mother more likely to believe Dora or Dan? Why? What effect might this have on Dora? On Dan?

3) Sandra, 14 years old, tells her best friend that her boyfriend raped her. Her friend doesn't want to listen. Act out how Sandra feels, both about the rape and about the indifference of her friend. Think about why the friend may not want to listen. Act that out.

4) A police officer pulls Arthur out of class and questions him about an accusation that he molested the neighbor child. How does Arthur feel being pulled out of class, what he does he think the other students will think of him, and how does he feel about being caught? What do you think the police officer might be thinking about Arthur and this situation? Act that out.

5) Jack is 8 years old. He was playing alone at the park playground just before dinner time when a man appeared with his tee-shirt over his face and masturbated in front of Jack. Jack was so afraid he could barely move, but he finally managed to run home. His father is angry at him for going to the park alone and for coming home late. Jack wants to tell him what happened but is afraid to, because he thinks he is to blame because he disobeyed. Role play Jack and his father. Have Jack finally tell what happened. What do Jack and his father feel at the beginning of their talk? At the end?

6) Ben was forcibly sodomized by an older and bigger man who worked at the same gas station where Ben used to work. Ben reported the offense, quit his job, and hadn't seen the man since; however, Ben's family has received threatening phone calls. Now Ben must testify at the offender's trial. Ben is standing outside the courtroom with his mother just before court when he sees his victimizer staring at them. Have Ben talk to his mother and his mother to Ben about the trial and about how both of them are feeling. Use lots of expression in your body and face.

Did this exercise help you empathize more deeply with what the characters were feeling? If not, try the scenario again. Switch roles, change your lines, and really get into your part. Discuss your character's feelings with the group. Did you really understand what your character was feeling?

Often sexual abuse victims write letters to their offenders as a part of their therapy. It helps them express the feelings they have about the offense and offenders. Most of these letters are not mailed. On the next page is a letter written by a young woman rape victim to a multiple rapist in prison for life after he had written an apology letter to her. It shows some of the intensity of a victim's feelings. (Also re-read the letter from the molestation victim to her molesting father in Chapter Eight.)

Dear Rapist,

So you've found God at this point in your life. You're now able to put your past behind you. Now you believe you've become a better person – according to who? God?

I can't understand how you can feel sorry for yourself. You can rape not only my body but my mind, use me for your own needs, then throw me away as if I were trash. Say you're sorry, sorry for what? Sorry for making my mind feel crazy, my body feel like scum, for making me afraid of the dark, not being able to go out alone. For not being able to enjoy sex because I find it sickening, nor being able to go near a closed door once it's dark, or enjoy a really good night's sleep.

You've taken so much from me. You've taken my independence, my security, my boldness, my toughness. You've insulted my integrity. Which one would you like to be sorry for?

The only one you feel sorry for is yourself, not me, and only because you are locked up. I too am a prisoner in my own mind. I can't seem to escape.

What gave you the right to inflict such ugliness on me? Did it make you feel tough, important, a big shot to your friends? And for what reason? Just to see if you could find such a person as myself and get away with it? You didn't think about how I felt. You could never know what you are putting me through.

The more I write, the more I get pissed off at you. I hope you rot in hell!

A Survivor

The next exercise in this chapter is another letter writing exercise, but this time it is a make-believe letter from your victim to you. Read the instructions carefully. Then sit down and complete the exercise.

EXERCISE 40. LETTER FROM YOUR VICTIM

Pretend you are your victim. Write a letter to yourself as if it came from your victim or your victim's parent. It should say what the victim would probably say to you if he/she wrote you a letter. It should cover:

a) How the victim felt about the offense at the time

b) How the victim feels now

c) How the victim feels about you

d) What resolution or outcome the victim would like to see

e) Anything else you think the victim would want to say to you. Think this through carefully. Make some notes first, then write the letter. Use extra paper if needed.

Notes: ______________________ ______________________

______________________ ______________________

______________________ ______________________

______________________ ______________________

______________________ ______________________

______________________ ______________________

Now write your letter.

Dear ______________________________*(your name)*:

____

____

____

____

____

____

____

____

____

____

____

____

____

____

____

____

____

____

____

____

____

____

Your victim

Another good exercise is to draw a picture of your victim's face. What emotion was on the face of your victim at the time of the offense? Now? Draw it. This exercise is another way of getting in touch with what your victim possibly feels and felt when you offended.

In many programs, as a part of the empathy building and restitution process, a lot of time is spent writing and discussing in group an apology letter from you to your victim. You can learn from this whether your counselor lets you send the letter or not. The point is to make sure you really acknowledge your offense, understand how the victim must have felt and feels now, understand the damage you have done, and can make a truly genuine apology for your offending behavior.

Therefore, for our final exercise of this chapter, you are to write an apology letter to your victim. The purpose is not to make you feel worse about what you did, but to help you take full responsibility and have full understanding so you will never do a similar act again.

EXERCISE 41. APOLOGY LETTER

Write a letter of apology to your victim (most recent victim if there is more than one). This letter should include:

1) An acknowledgment of your offense (taking full responsibility for it, including a clarification that the victim did not cause the offense)

2) An acknowledgment of how you set up and tricked the victim

3) A statement showing full awareness of the harm you did to the victim

4) A statement showing understanding of the emotions you put the victim through

5) A sincere apology for committing the offense

6) An explanation of why, to the best of your knowledge, you did what you did

7) An explanation of how you have made sure you will never commit an offense again. (Use extra paper if you do not have enough space here.)

Dear ____________________(your victim's first name):

____

____

____

____

____

____

____

____

____

____

____

____

____

____

____

____

____

____

____

____

____

____________________(your signature)

The important thing now is to remember *before* you commit a sex offense what your potential victims feel. It is particularly important to remember the harm done to victims when you are at the *Lapse* point in your offending chain, when you start thinking about offending. Yell "STOP" to your fantasies about offending and replace them with thoughts of the damage you will do to the victim. When you see a potential victim, think about that potential victim as a person, not an object to be used. Really think about the harm you will do to that person if you offend. Remind yourself that you are a good person who helps, not hurts, people. Plan ways to get your needs satisfied in ways that won't hurt anyone. (Review the better ways to satisfy your needs that you listed in Exercise 23 in Chapter Five.)

SUMMARY

In this chapter, you have:

1) Learned what empathy means
2) Increased your awareness of what other people feel in general
3) Increased your awareness of what sexual abuse victims feel in particular
4) Gained an understanding of how people react similarly but differently to the same or similar situations
5) Learned about some of the common thinking errors or distortions offenders make
6) Gotten more in touch with what your victim was thinking and feeling
7) Taken responsibility and apologized for what you did
8) Learned where and how you can use empathy to prevent reoffense

NOTES

CHAPTER TEN

COMMUNICATION

Improving communication is a critical part of your Relapse Prevention plan. The dictionary defines *communication* as "a process by which information is exchanged between individuals through a common system of symbols, signs or behavior." In simpler terms, communication means sharing information with other people either with written or spoken words or by physical gestures (such as shrugging your shoulders to say "I don't know") and behaviors. Communication has three parts: verbal expression, nonverbal expression, and reception (listening).

Verbal expression simply means using words to express your thoughts and feelings. These words can be spoken or written. They can also be direct or indirect. For example, when you tell somebody something or write them a letter, that is direct verbal communication. When you write a play or poem, or talk to someone other than the person to whom the communication is directed, these are forms of indirect verbal communication.

Nonverbal expression means using some way other than words to express yourself, for example, body language – the expression on your face or the position of your shoulders or hands can tell others how you are feeling. If you are feeling sad, usually your face will look unhappy, your shoulders are more likely to be slumped, your hands will either be hanging dejectedly or possibly clenched against your body to close others out, and your walk may be kind of slow and draggy. If you are feeling happy, on the other hand, you are likely to have a smile on your face, stand straighter, and walk with more energy.

Other types of nonverbal communication are things you do, or behaviors, such as hitting something or someone or kissing a special friend. Those are direct nonverbal communications, while other things you might do, such as art work or sports, tell someone what you are thinking and feeling indirectly.

When you committed your sex offense, you were communicating. Think about what you were communicating, both emotions and thoughts. Who were you communicating with? Was it verbal or nonverbal or some of both? Was this direct or indirect communication? Who should your message *really* have been directed to? How could you communicate this message in a non-hurtful way?

For example, a 13-year-old boy named Hank felt he was always being blamed by his stepfather for things his two younger stepsisters did. He punished Hank for breaking a vase even though his stepsisters had knocked it off the table while running through the house. Hank was very angry. His mother worked long hours and was not around to talk to, and his stepfather punished him more for "talking back" when Hank tried to explain. Hank felt angry, trapped, and powerless. He communicated these feelings in an indirect, destructive way by violently raping his two stepsisters. He wasn't aware he was communicating anything. He was acting out his anger, frustration, and feelings of powerlessness on his stepsisters and getting a kind of revenge against his stepfather. He was indirectly and nonverbally telling him "I'm furious at you and your daughters. I will get some kind of power and control over this situation."

Communication can be healthy or unhealthy. For example, when you scream and swear at people or call them names, the communication is not a healthy one. When you talk out your problems and feelings, it is healthy. When you punch somebody or punch the wall and hurt your hand, you are expressing yourself in an unhealthy, unproductive way. But when you write down your feelings or draw them or even jog or do other physical exercise to express them, your actions will help you resolve your feelings.

When you use positive ways to communicate your thoughts and feelings you are less likely to reoffend. You will develop a healthy, productive way to deal with the situations you face without moving down the *Offense Chain* to *Relapse* (offending).

The following exercise is designed to help you choose and practice healthy communication.

EXERCISE 42. HEALTHY AND UNHEALTHY COMMUNICATION

1) For each of the following situations, write down whether communication was healthy or unhealthy and why.

a) Jody's older brother made fun of her all the time. She went to him one day and told him how bad it made her feel. Was this healthy or unhealthy?_______ Why?________________________________

____

b) Don got blamed for something someone else did at school. The teacher wouldn't listen to him when he tried to explain, so he wrote a letter to the teacher and explained the situation. Was this healthy or unhealthy? Why? ____

____

c) Richie's father yelled at him, so he yelled back. Was this healthy or unhealthy? ______________
Why? ____

d) John's stepmother was always hollering at him. He felt like he couldn't talk to her so he put a garter snake in her bed. Was this healthy or unhealthy? _____ Why?________________________________

____

e) Andy's father was a drug user who was sent to prison. Andy was angry at his father, but his mother would not let him write a letter to his father to let him know how he felt. Andy drew a picture of his father, punched it in the nose, stomped on it and crumpled it up. Was this healthy or unhealthy? ______________
Why? ____

When Andy's father got out of prison, Andy did the same thing in person. He punched his father and kicked him. Was this healthy or unhealthy? _________ Why?________________________________

____

f) Ricardo's uncle molested him when he was 7 years old. His uncle denied it. Ricardo felt enraged, frustrated, and powerless. He went to the gym and boxed. Was this healthy or unhealthy? ______________
Why? ____

If Ricardo had punched his biggest enemy at school instead, would that have been healthy? __________
Why or why not? ____

g) Gina's father slept around with all kinds of women. Gina knew about it and hated it. She wrote a letter to her father in which she called her father an oversexed baboon. Was this healthy or unhealthy? _________

Why? ____

h) Roger felt that his parents never listened to him. He was feeling depressed and misunderstood. He went into his room and stayed there, thinking over and over that nobody cared about him. He didn't want to talk to anybody. Was this healthy or unhealthy? ______ Why?___________________________________

____

i) Don had the urge to expose himself. He never spoke of it. Was this healthy or unhealthy?___________

Why? ____

j) Miguel was thinking about what it would feel like to touch the breasts of his friend's 7-year-old sister. He talked to his older brother about what he was feeling. Was this healthy or unhealthy? ___________

Why? ____

If, instead, he had talked to the 7-year-old girl, would that have been healthy or unhealthy?___________

Why? ____

k) Mic played his guitar whenever he felt frustrated. Was this healthy or unhealthy?___________

Why? ____

2) For the following situations, write down a healthy way the person could communicate his/her emotions and thoughts. It could be verbal or nonverbal, direct or indirect.

a) Maria's mother molested her. She didn't like what her mother did but she still loved her. Maria wanted her mother to know that she loved her but was very angry that her mother had hurt and betrayed her. Maria is not allowed to see her. How could she communicate these feelings?___________________________

____

____

b) Tom's aunt and uncle won't speak to him since he molested their daughter (his cousin). They got a restraining order so he is not even allowed write to them. How can he express his feelings of remorse and sadness?

____

____

c) Randy was expelled for fighting. The other boy hit him, and he didn't even hit back, but the assistant principal wouldn't listen to him or his witnesses. How can he communicate the true story? ___________

____

____

____

d) Maria is very attracted to Chad, but is not sure if he even knows she's alive. How can she communicate her feelings to him in a way where she wouldn't look stupid in case he doesn't like her? ___________

____

____

____

e) Alberto, age 12, goes to a school dance with a girl he likes. This is his first date. He wants to kiss her, but is not sure that she wants to. He is too embarrassed to ask her. How could he communicate what he wants to do and find out what she wants without coming out and asking her?

f) Penny is furious at her brother for taking off and leaving her without bus fare. She is afraid that if she talks to him she will fly off the handle. How can she communicate her feelings in a safe manner?

g) Don is feeling depressed and wonders if life is worth living. He would like some help but doesn't know how to ask for it. He is afraid people will think of him as a "weirdo" or "nerd" if he asks for help. How could he communicate his feelings and to whom?

h) Nick came home from football practice hurting and exhausted. He knows his mother is going insist that he get his chores done right away. He has laryngitis and can't talk. How can he show her how he feels and that he needs rest instead?

i) Rod starts a new school in a tough neighborhood. He wants to look strong and able to take care of himself. What body language would give that message?

j) Louis is feeling very frustrated at his group home. There is nobody he can talk to, and he is not good at expressing himself in writing. How else can he let his feelings out?

k) Jenny, a classmate of Bob's, likes Bob, but he isn't interested in dating her. How can he let her know he isn't interested in a relationship without hurting her feelings?

You can see in the first part of this exercise that communications that either hurt you or someone else are unhealthy. Usually not communicating is unhealthy also, but communicating to the wrong person, like the 7-year-old girl Miguel was fantasizing about in situation # 1-j, was even more unhealthy because it put him in a dangerous situation where he would be likely to reoffend. So, just as we learned in Chapter Five about the consequences of the choices we make, it is important to think about the consequences of communications.

The second part of the exercise shows you that there are many different ways you can express your thoughts and feelings. You have many choices in each of these situations. Did you think of talking to a third party or getting someone to help Randy in situation # 2-c? Did you think about body language in any of the other situations? What about other types of verbal and nonverbal communications?

In many of these situations, the person needed to assert him/herself. *Assertiveness* is something that is often misunderstood. People often mix up *assertiveness* with aggressiveness or anger. When you yell at someone in anger, you are not being *assertive*. *Assertiveness* is where you can make your needs, thoughts, or feelings known in a calm, convincing manner. For example, George wants his brother to get out of his room. If he yells, "Get the hell out of here," he is not being assertive. He is being aggressive, because he sounds threatening and is out of control. To be assertive, he would say, "Please leave my room. I'll respect your space if you respect mine." And, if his brother doesn't get out, he would repeat firmly, "I told you nicely to please leave my room."

One of the best ways to be *assertive* is to say what *you* are feeling rather than to criticize someone else. For example, if you don't like the way your boyfriend or girlfriend hangs on to you, it would be more assertive and effective to say, "I feel uncomfortable having you hold my arm, so please let go," rather than "You're always so possessive. Why do you always have to hang on to me?" The other person is much more likely to be hurt and get mad at you in the second case.

You can determine what is *assertive* and what is aggressive by the way you are feeling when you make certain statements and by the consequences. If you say something loudly and angrily or in a threatening way, you are most likely being aggressive. If you speak calmly and firmly, you are being *assertive*. If the person receiving the message feels attacked, what you said was probably aggressive. Judging by consequences is not always foolproof, but you can often guess what the reactions to what you are saying will be. Learn to temper your statements to communicate what you want without personally attacking someone.

The next exercise is a short one to help you distinguish between *assertiveness* and aggressiveness.

EXERCISE 43. ASSERTIVE VS. AGGRESSIVE

1) After each of the following statements write whether the statement was *aggressive* or *assertive*.

a) Joe's little brother is in his room again. He yells, "Get the hell out of here or I'll bust your face in." Aggressive or assertive? ________________________________

b) When his friend grabs Jim's letter from his girlfriend, Jim says strongly, "Give me that immediately." Aggressive or assertive? ________________________________

c) When the friend starts to read it, Jim repeats, "Give me the letter back immediately," and adds "if you want to stay friends." Aggressive or assertive? ________________________________

d) When Maria wants Alex to stop touching her breasts, she says firmly, "I want you to stop touching me right now." Aggressive or assertive? ______

e) When Alex doesn't stop, Maria repeats what she said and adds, "If you don't, I will never go out with you again. I mean it." Aggressive or assertive? ______

f) When he still doesn't stop, Maria adds, "If you don't stop, I will file a criminal complaint against you." Aggressive or assertive? ______

g) If Maria had said instead, "You son-of-a-----, you think you're God's gift to women. Well, you're nothing but a two-bit punk, and I'm going to make sure you get locked up for this!" Aggressive or assertive? ______

______

h) Bill's little brother messed up their room looking for an old shirt in Bill's dresser. Bill yells, "You jerk. You messed up all my stuff. Keep your mitts out of my drawers." Aggressive or assertive? ______

______

i) Carla wants her brother to turn down the TV so she can study. She asks him nicely, but her brother doesn't respond, so she yells, "Are you deaf? Turn down the damn TV." Aggressive or assertive? ______

______

j) Dave's girlfriend Sharyn is always telling her friends how cute David's "buns" are. This is very embarrassing to him. He says to her, "It really bothers me when you talk about my behind. I want you to stop." Aggressive or assertive? ______

______

k) When Sharyn says she will say anything she wants to, Dave says to her, "If you continue, I'll just tell everyone how your brother molested you." Assertive or aggressive? ______
Why? ______

l) When Ed finds out his friend has brought drugs into Ed's car, which is a no-no to Ed, Ed says, "I'm afraid I can't drive you anywhere any more, because you put my license in jeopardy by breaking my rules." Assertive or aggressive? ______

______

______

m) If Ed had said instead, "You punk, don't you ever listen to anyone? You know the rules, now get the hell out of my car." Assertive or aggressive? ______

______

2) In the following section change the aggressive statements quoted to assertive ones instead

a) Father says to his son who has done an incomplete job on the lawn, "Can't you do anything right? The lawn is still a mess." ______

______

b) Frank says to his younger brother who wants to tag along, "Why would I want some dopey little kid tagging along? Get out of my sight." ______

______

c) To a friend who forgot to return a tape, Terry says, "You knew I needed the tape. Can't you remember anything?" ______

______

d) To a guy who keeps pestering her, Holly says, "Get away from me, you dumb jerk." ______

______

e) To his sister who changed the channel he was watching on TV when he answered the phone, Ike says, "Get your slimy hands off my TV. You knew I was watching the game."____________________

____

f) Jerry has to share a locker with a classmate who is messy. Jerry yells, "You slob. Can't you put anything away where it belongs?" ____________________________

____

g) When Kim's mother blames him for what his brother Jeff did for the tenth time, Kim yells, "You always pick on me. You like Jeff better. I wish you were dead." ________________________

____

h) When LouAnn's boyfriend pays more attention to another girl at a party, she wants him to stop, so she says, "You don't even care about me. I wish I had never met you."____________________

____

3) Now, think of a time when you said something aggressively to someone. Write down what it was and what the situation was.

Situation: ____________________________________

____

What you said: ________________________________

What is an assertive statement you could have made instead? ____________________

____

After making your assertive statement, if you don't get the response you want, it is important to make the same statement again even more strongly. Always look at what you are trying to accomplish with your statement. Do your best not to hurt the person's feelings if you can avoid it. Even people who act obnoxious have feelings. Often they feel truly bad about themselves and cover the feelings up by being obnoxious. Can you think of anyone like that? (Most of us know someone.)

Telling someone what you want or would like to have happen is often more difficult than criticizing the actions of someone else. A positive example of *assertiveness* would be where one of your friends asks another of your friends to go to the show on Saturday. You would like to go too. You have a choice whether or not to assert yourself. If you don't say what you want, for sure you won't get to go with them. If you whine, "You never ask me to do anything," instead of asserting yourself, you are likely to be misunderstood and disliked. But if you say, "May I join you?" you have positively asserted yourself. While you may face the possibility of rejection by asking in an appropriately assertive manner, it is worth the chance. (Even if you are told no, you have other options, such as asking other friends to go, going by yourself, going bowling, or going to a video arcade instead. The rejection may have nothing to do with their liking or disliking you. Use your positive self-talk. Tell yourself, "Maybe his Dad said he could only take one person with him," "There may not be room in the car," or "Maybe he owes John the favor, because John took him last week.")

Telling someone what you *don't* want is also difficult, particularly if you are not sure what is going on with the other person. This is what happens in many molestation cases. The victim may feel sort of funny – not sure of whether what the more powerful person wants is okay or not. The victim doesn't say "no," because he/she is afraid of offending the more powerful person, who is usually someone the victim likes or respects. Can you think of a situation where you felt funny saying "no?" Did you ever say "yes," when you really meant "no," because you didn't want to displease the person who asked you?

When people say "yes" when they really want to say "no," usually they feel angry at the other person for talking them into doing something they don't want to to do and angry at themselves for letting it happen. This anger and resentment can lead to aggression when it builds up over time.

An example of this is Louie. He and his friends were at a party. His friends were smoking crack and said, "Come on Louie, are you chicken?" Louie didn't want to smoke crack, but he was afraid his friends wouldn't like him if he didn't try it. So, instead of saying "no," he went ahead and smoked it with them. Afterward, Louie felt like he had no backbone. He was mad at himself and his friends for putting him in that situation.

Another example is 14-year-old Mickey, who hadn't yet had a girlfriend. Mickey's friends always bragged about the sexual things they had done with their girlfriends. His friend Frankie arranged for him to meet a girl at the show the next evening. Frankie said, "Put your arm around her, then put your hand on her breast." Mickey felt uncomfortable about putting his hand on the girl's breast, but he did it anyway because he was afraid Frankie and his other friends would think he was a baby. The girl was upset. Mickey felt angry with himself because he listened to Frankie's advice instead of standing up for himself and what he felt.

It is important to say what you feel, and best to say it directly to the person involved (unless that puts your life in danger). There is some risk: some people don't like it or feel threatened when you say what you are feeling or refuse to go along; but others will respect you for standing up for yourself. Most important is that when you say what you really feel and make your own positive, healthy choices, you can feel good about yourself and respect yourself.

Communicating in healthy ways and being assertive take practice. It's not easy, and you don't always get what you want even when you make clear, calm, assertive statements. But the more you communicate well, the more likely that you'll feel better about yourself, and maybe even get some things to happen the way you want them to. When both people in a situation are assertive, there can be a compromise that helps both participants.

It is okay to say "no" when you feel that way. You will feel better afterward. Louie could have said, "Count me out. It's not my thing," or "Half my family are addicts and alcoholics. I don't want to end up like them." Maybe his friends (if in fact they were his friends) would have just said, "Okay, dude, but you don't know what you're missing," and still think he's okay.

If Mickey had stood up to Frankie and said, "I'd like to get to know her, but I'd rather move at my own speed and hers," and hadn't followed Frankie's advice, Frankie might have thought Mickey was slow, or even not interested in girls. But Mickey would be able to keep the girl as a friend afterward, and would know more about whether he really wanted Frankie as a friend.

You should be aware, however, that it is hard – almost impossible – for little children to tell a big person they love or respect to stop molesting them, and often the big person ignores what they say. Did your victim say "no" to you? If so, did you listen and stop? Remember, the third part of communication is reception (listening).

Just like some people say "yes" when they mean "no," other people say "no" when they really mean "yes." For example, Manuel was very shy and had never gone out with any girls before. Nora, one of the most popular girls at school, asked him to a party. He wanted to go, but he was worried – afraid he would be the only Hispanic kid there and not fit in, afraid he would look strange or say something other people would think was weird, so he told Nora he couldn't. Afterward, he was angry at himself for giving in to his fears. He missed what might have been a really good time, because he was afraid to say "yes."

Don't confuse this with someone saying "no" in a sexual situation. When someone says "no" in a sexual situation, you need to believe that the person means it. You can ask the other person to talk about his or her feelings, but when it comes to sex, NO means NO. Even when someone has mixed feelings, it is safer for you to take this as a "no." This section is about you saying "yes" or "no" for yourself only. It is important to honor other people's yes and no.

The next exercise looks at the problem of yes and no.

EXERCISE 44. SAYING WHAT YOU MEAN: YES AND NO

1) Think of a time when you said "yes" when you really meant "no." Write down the situation, how you felt at the time, and how you felt afterward.

Situation: ____________________

____

____

How you felt at the time you said "yes:" ____________________

____

How you felt afterward: ____________________

____

2) Think of a time you said "no" when you really wanted to say "yes."

Situation: ____________________

____

____

What kept you from expressing what you really meant?____________________

____

____

3) List four situations where you would like to say "no," but have difficulty with it. Tell why.

a) Situation: ____________________

Reason: ____________________

b) Situation: ____________________

Reason: ____________________

c) Situation: ____________________

Reason: ____________________

d) Situation: ____________________

Reason: ____________________

4) Can you think of a situation now where you are afraid to say "yes" when you really want to? ____________

____

____

5) Why will you feel better about yourself when you say what you really mean and want?____________

____

____

6) Tell what you would say and what reason you would give to say "yes" or "no" in the following situations:

a) You are best friends with Mack. He asks you to help him cheat on a test. You don't want to. How would you tell him "no?" Give your reasoning to him in the answer.____________

____

b) Joanie, a girl who is a good friend of yours, asks you to a dance. You only like her as a friend and don't want to go with her, but you are afraid of hurting her feelings if you say "no." Assert yourself and tell her wh

____

____

c) Your best friend asks you to go on vacation with him. You don't like to be with his parents, because they get drunk and abusive. You know he wants you to come, but you don't want to. How can you tell him?____

____

____

d) Pete, your best friend, asks to borrow money from you. You don't have any to spare, and, besides, he never paid you back the last loan he got from you. How do you tell him "no?" ____________

____

e) Your boss asks you to stay late at work. You will get into trouble at home if you do, but you also are worried that he will fire you if you don't stay. How can you say "no?"____________

____

____

f) Your best friend asks you out to dinner at a very fancy restaurant. You would like to go, but are afraid you will feel uncomfortable. How can you say "yes," but let your friend know your fears? ____________

____

g) Make up a scene from your own life where you could have asserted yourself and said "no" or "yes" and act it out in your treatment group with another person.

People communicate nonverbally, that is, without words. Have you ever known that your mom was feeling fed-up and angry before she ever said a word? Or that a good friend felt bummed out about something before he/she ever said anything? Have you ever smashed a wall to get your anger out? Or thrown something on the ground? These examples all show nonverbal communication.

Every now and then we see people whose body language or facial expression is out of step with what is going on. This is very confusing, and makes us generally wonder about them. For example, Shawn's pet dog died and Shawn smiled while talking about it. Sometimes people who have closed off their emotions act this way, including many people who have been abused.

Sometimes children smile or laugh when they are being scolded by a parent or teacher. Usually it is not because they think it is funny, but because they're nervous or would rather laugh than let anyone know they're upset enough to cry. Smiling is a way of trying to keep anyone from knowing that the criticism hurts them. It is out of step with their real feelings. Often adults don't understand and punish them because they think the child is showing disrespect, or not taking the situation seriously. Has this ever happened to you?

If you can, and if it doesn't put you in physical danger, it is better to allow yourself to show with your body and face exactly what you are feeling. People relate more with people who communicate in body language as well as words.

People also communicate what they want or don't want through body language and facial expressions. For example, if someone is attracted to you, he/she may show you this without words, by making eye contact, giving you looks, hanging out near you, and so forth. If someone *doesn't* like you, he or she is likely to move away and look away.

It is important to read other people's body language and facial expressions. Do you remember what the expression was on your victim's face when you were sexually abusing him/her? What about your victim's body language? Did the victim turn or pull away, look frozen, or hunch over in fear? Picture it in your mind. Draw a picture of your victim's face. This is one way to get in touch with what your victim might have been feeling and communicating nonverbally. Try it.

Some good exercises you can do in group to practice non-verbal communication are called *Communication Charades*.

EXERCISE 45. COMMUNICATION CHARADES

1) Write out 20 different emotion words each on a separate small piece of paper. (You can refer to the list of feeling words in Chapter Four.) Fold the papers in half, so nobody can see what is on them. Take turns with one person at a time picking an emotion and acting it out. The others in the group will guess what it is. Keep track of the time it took for each person to act out the emotion well enough for the others to guess it. Each person should do several emotion words. Whoever has the lowest time wins.

2) Divide into twos. Each team picks an emotion and develops a scene in which one or both of the persons would feel that emotion. They can use words, but not any emotion words to act out their scene. The audience then has to guess what emotion they have communicated indirectly through their scene. For example, if the word is "joy," you might have them talking about winning the lottery and jumping up and down. Use the same timing system to determine the winning team.

3) Write the following messages on separate pieces of paper. Have each person pick a message. Don't let anyone else see them. Have one person at a time act out without words the message he/she picked. Again, keep a record of the time it took the others to guess what that person was trying to say.

a) Leave me alone. ____________________
b) I want to make love to you. ____________________
c) Go away. ____________________
d) Come here. ____________________
e) Stop that. ____________________
f) Please take me with you. ____________________
g) Don't hurt me. ____________________
h) What time is it? ____________________
i) Let's play. ____________________
j) I've got to study. ____________________

Think up additional messages of your own, too. ______________________________

____

____

____

____

____

____

____

____

____

____

If someone smiles and looks happy while he is saying, "My dog died last night, " you would understand that the dog died by the words he said, but be confused by his facial expression and body language. You would wonder why he would be happy about the dog dying, or probably make a judgment that this person is really out of touch with his feelings. When sex offenders begin treatment, often they show no feelings about their offenses. They may say, "I feel terrible about hurting my sister," but give no appearances of regret. Probation officers, in particular, often pick up on this. Have you had a probation officer who wrote, "...does not show remorse," or a similar comment in your probation report?

After all the work you have done on emotions, empathy, and communication, you are probably now in better touch with your feelings and better able to communicate them both verbally and nonverbally, directly and indirectly. Try saying the words, "I am very sorry," first when you really *feel* sorry. Express your sorrow in your face and body. Then say the same thing, but think to yourself, "I'm not really sorry at all. I'm just saying this because I have to." Show how you feel this time in your facial expression and how you hold your body. If you are really doing this well, people should be able to tell how you are feeling as well as hear what you are saying.

Did anyone ever say to you, "You're not really sorry." Were you sorry? Or were you just faking it because you didn't want to accept the consequences? If you were sorry, you probably didn't communicate very well nonverbally.

This leads us into the next portion of our *Communication* chapter: receiving the message. For every thought or feeling to be communicated, there must be someone who is listening or receiving it. *Reception* is probably the most important aspect of communication. It is also the one that most people practice least. It is particularly important for you, as a sex offender, to be very aware of what others are communicating, especially potential victims. If you had really been aware of what your victim was trying to communicate to you, either in words or body language, you might have chosen not to offend.

Often, teenagers who begin treatment have difficulty really listening to what others say, perhaps because they need attention and have not learned to listen well. Does this describe you? Really make an effort to listen. It is extremely important.

When we listen, we receive information on two levels, the *thought* level and the *feeling* level. For example, John's girlfriend invites him to a rock concert. He loves her but he hates heavy metal music. He might say, "I would be glad to go with you," meaning he is willing to go, but underneath she can sense that on the feeling level, he doesn't really want to go.

To understand both what people are saying *and* what they are feeling when they transmit a message to you, it is necessary to watch body language, hear vocal inflections, and notice facial expressions as well as listening to the words a person is saying. Just as healthy expressive communication requires that you use good verbal and nonverbal skills, reception or listening requires that you use your eyes as well as your ears.

Do the next exercise in group or with a partner. It will give you an opportunity to both express yourself in words and body language *and* receive messages on the thought and emotional levels.

EXERCISE 46. GIVING AND RECEIVING COMMUNICATIONS

Part 1. Thought level: In group, pair up, then tell the other person all about one of the most embarrassing things that ever happened to you – when it happened, where you were, who was there, what happened, and why you were so embarrassed. When you finish, have the person repeat the facts back to you. Did the person fully understand what you said? Correct any differences or misconceptions. Then trade places and ask the other person to tell you all about one of the most embarrassing things that ever happened to him or her.

(You can also do this exercise in a circle, where you tell the person next to you, who tells the person next to him or her what you said, then that person tells the person next to him or her what you said, and so on, until the last person tells you. You then tell the last person how accurate the final recounting is and correct the differences. The group also figures out where the story changed. This is a variation on the children's game where you whisper something into the first person's ear.)

Try this exercise with other life experiences, like the most important day of your life, the most exciting time you ever had, the worst thing that ever happened to you, and so forth.

Part 2. Feeling level: (there are two sections to this part).

A) This exercise is similar to the last, but the emotional content is not known in advance.

Tell another person about a school experience you had. Tell yourself in your head what you were feeling about this experience, but don't tell the other person out loud. As you talk about the time, place, people involved, and what happened, let your feelings be known through your vocal inflection, facial expression and body language. Do not exaggerate. When you finish, the person will tell you the basic facts of the story and what it appeared that you were feeling at the time. Discuss how accurate the person was regarding both the thought and feeling content of the story.

Also do this exercise with happenings at home, camp, vacation, church, sports, concerts, and so forth.

B) In this part of the exercise you can either break into pairs, or do it as though you were playing charades in a group setting. Say each of the following phrases, in a way that expresses one of the feelings written after it. The other person or group must guess which of the feelings you were expressing.

"I'm furious"	joking	upset	sarcastic
"I love you"	with love	hateful	teasing
"You stink"	joking	smelly	angry
"I'm sorry"	sincere	angry	afraid
"I feel sick"	disgusted	ill, unwell	bored
"I'm lost"	frightened	angry	sarcastic
"I'll miss you"	sad	flirtatious	angry

"My name is"..	friendly	angry	as a sexual come-on
"Who are you?"..	curious	threatening	afraid
"What do you want?"...............................	nervous	curious	angry
"I don't understand"................................	confused	hurt	angry
"I'm through"..	done	disgusted	sad
"You're cute"..	sexy	admiring	disgusted
"You goofed"..	angry	laughing	weary
"I'm afraid"...	terrified	sarcastic	worried

Make up additional phrases of your own and different ways to express them.

The best way to learn to express yourself and receive communications from others is to *use* the various types of communication. This means practicing good communication. Practice at home, at school, everywhere you go. Say what you are thinking and feeling, and listen and watch what other people are trying to say to you.

Good communication is necessary for all types of relationships. It is critical to your success in love relationships, at work settings, at school, at home, in recreational situations, and so forth.

SUMMARY

You had the opportunity to learn about the following aspects of communication:

1) That communication includes both verbal and nonverbal expression
2) That communication can be both direct and indirect
3) How to distinguish between healthy and unhealthy communication
4) More ways of communicating in a healthy manner
5) The difference between assertiveness and aggressiveness
6) How to be assertive and say what you mean
7) How to communicate by facial expression and body language
8) The importance of your facial expressions and body language showing what you mean
9) The importance of listening well (reception)
10) Awareness of listening on both the thought and feeling levels
11) The need to use one's eyes as well as ears in listening (receiving messages)
12) How the same phrase can have different meanings depending on how it is expressed

CHAPTER ELEVEN

SEX, LOVE, AND FRIENDSHIP

These three important topics – sex, love, and friendship – we combined in this chapter because most sex offenders tend to lump them together, even though they are very different categories. It's no wonder that sex is mixed up with everything! It is used for different purposes and combined with just about every possible subject in many different contexts. Advertisements, in particular, use sex to sell perfumes, sodas, blue jeans, cars, and almost anything else you can think of.

SEX

Sex is described in the dictionary as "the instinct or attraction drawing one sex toward another, or its manifestation in sexual behavior." Sex involves your brain, all your physical senses and your genitals. As with other choices you make, the choice to have sex results in both positive and negative consequences. The positive consequences include sexual release, good feelings, and (for adults who are ready to be parents) babies; the negative consequences include babies (for people too young to be good parents), abortions, reputations, and sexually transmitted diseases, such as herpes, syphilis, chlamydia, and HIV or AIDS. Some of the negative consequences can be prevented when both partners take responsibility by using birth control *and* a condom.

Sex may exist together with love and/or friendship or completely separately. When people consent to have sex together without being in a committed relationship, it is usually called "casual sex." Casual sex is what you have probably already been involved in, sex just to have sex, just for orgasms, without caring about the other person. Casual sex may be physically pleasant, but it does not satisfy your needs for closeness and caring. If you are in a relationship with a boyfriend or girlfriend, having casual sex with someone else means you are probably violating your boy/girlfriend's trust. Frequent casual sex often means that the person has a problem with intimacy and/or was sexually abused.

Responsible sex involves caring about the other person as much as you care about yourself. It involves a relationship of respect and trust. It allows both partners to share their feelings as well as their genitals. It requires consideration of the consequences. Responsible sex means using birth control *and* a condom.

When a person has a sexual experience with someone without their consent, or with someone who is underage and/or not able to consent, he/she has hurt someone and has committed a sex offense. Sex offenses are crimes. There are also sex offenses that don't involve touching. Obscene phone calls, exposing one's genitals, prowling, peeping, taking nude or sexy photos, or showing a child pornography are sex offenses just like the hands-on offenses such as rape and touching a child's private parts.

People who commit sex offenses often confuse sex with other qualities, like intimacy (closeness and caring) or power. Confusing sex with intimacy often happens when the offenders were molested themselves when they were young, felt some closeness during the sexual connection they had with their perpetrators, and mistakenly think having sex will bring them the intimacy they are looking for. But it doesn't. While the victim may feel some pleasurable bodily sensations, feelings of being used, powerless, or dirty combine with them. Not only does the offender *not* get the intimacy he or she wants, but the victim is emotionally harmed.

When Isabel was little, her favorite uncle molested her. Although she felt kind of dirty and used afterward, she still really loved her uncle. She confused her feelings of closeness to him with her sexual experience. When Isabel was 15 years old, she felt lonely and unloved. She didn't have many friends. She babysat her 8-year-old cousin Eddy every week. He really loved her, because she played with him and listened to him. One day she had him touch her breasts. She then had him pull down his pants and she rubbed his penis. She was trying to find the closeness she thought she had with her uncle. She didn't think about the effect it would have on Eddy, who was confused and hurt. She felt ashamed and guilty afterward, and still felt lonely and unloved. In addition, she was arrested. She had acted out her need for intimacy and love in an inappropriate, illegal, sexual way with someone who could not understand and consent. She had confused love and intimacy with sex.

Power is another quality people who sexually offend confuse with sex. When you feel powerless and inadequate, sometimes frustrated too, you want to gain control of somebody or something. Perpetrators who sexually assault or molest someone who is weaker or younger, expose their genitals to a stranger, peep or make obscene phone calls, or rape someone, often are trying to satisfy their need for power by misusing sex.

Rocky's father was extremely critical and strict. Rocky felt like he could never do anything right. There was no way he could please his father, and it made him feel powerless. He and his friends had made some prank phone calls to people they knew and felt powerful for doing them. One day, Rocky misdialed the phone and a strange woman answered. Instead of hanging up, Rocky found himself saying all kinds of sexual things to her. The woman sounded afraid and hung up. Rocky felt powerful. He had the power to scare her and the sexual talk excited him. He began to call lots of random numbers in the phone book and say more and more sexual and sexually violent things. Eventually he was caught when a young woman asked the police to put a trap on her phone and the call was traced. Rocky was using sex improperly to substitute for power, and he was arrested because the way he did it harmed the people he did it to and was illegal.

Other ways people misuse sex are as an outlet for anger (as a way of getting out the anger the person is feeling onto someone else sexually, as in rape), an outlet for excitement (as a way of getting away from the boredom and humdrum parts of life), and an outlet for tension (through the physical release during climax). These are just a few of the reasons offenders mix up sex with the satisfaction of another emotion. Can you figure out what was behind your misuse of sex?

LOVE

Love is described in the dictionary as "a profoundly tender, passionate affection for another person" or "a feeling of warm personal attachment or deep affection." It does not require a sexual relationship. Most people love their parents or other family members. Sex is not appropriate with family members. When sex is a part of a love relationship, it is an additional intimate physical experience adding to the love relationship, and should be with an appropriate, similar age partner who feels the same way.

There are various qualities people look for in a love relationship. These include not just what a person looks like (we are all initially attracted to people we think are handsome or beautiful), but also characteristics like warmth, or trust, or liking the same things. Everyone has a slightly different list of what is important to him/her in a love relationship. The next exercise will give you the opportunity to explore what is important to you in a love relationship.

EXERCISE 47. LOVE AND SEX QUALITIES

Part 1. Love: The following list consists of qualities lots of people look for in love relationships with a partner. Read them over. Add any additional ones that are important to you.

Check all the ones that are important to you. Double check the ones that are most important.

Attractive/good looking ______ Sexy looking ______ Smart ______
Friendly ______ Outgoing ______ Loving ______
Fun to be with ______ Caring ______ Honest ______
Trustworthy ______ Rich ______ Sensitive ______
Attentive ______ Easy to be with ______ Popular ______
Likes the same things ______ Likes sex ______ Good kisser ______
Smells good ______ Good worker ______ Kind ______
Good sense of humor ______ Big breasts ______ Big penis ______
Muscular ______ Cute ass ______ Tattoos ______
Needy/insecure ______ Shy ______ Strong ______
Bold/assertive ______ Quiet ______ Rowdy ______
Communicates well ______ Reliable ______ Independent ______
Understanding ______ In tune with my thoughts and feelings ______
Willing to compromise ______ Exciting ______ Affectionate ______
Mature ______ Old fashioned ______ With it ______
Other ______

Part 2. Sex: Now look at the qualities that turn you on sexually. These are triggers which physically arouse you, that is, make your body feel very sexually excited. Are some of these triggers among the words in the list above? Write down these qualities and any others that cause you to be sexually attracted to a person on the lines below.

There are probably a lot of the characteristics that appear on both your love relationship and sex lists. People are usually sexually attracted to people with whom they would like to have a long-term love relationship. Sometimes, however, a person may want a sexual fling with someone who excites him/her, but doesn't want to have a long-term love relationship with that individual. Does that happen for you? Once again, if it is consensual and understood between two parties of similar age and ability, this is not illegal, but often one of the parties feels more deeply than the other and can be emotionally hurt.

Homosexuality – being gay or lesbian – means that you are closest to and most comfortable in sexual relationships with people of the same sex as you. There is some controversy about whether people's sexual orientation (heterosexual or homosexual) is genetically or biochemically determined (whether they are "born that way"), or whether it is formed during their lifetime. Either way, for many people these preferences are well established before they start school.

Many people have learned thinking errors about homosexuality. Their thinking errors are usually based on an irrational fear of homosexuality. That fear is called homophobia. Homosexuals are no different from anyone else except that they are more attracted to persons of the same sex than to persons of the opposite sex.

One way of thinking about sexuality is as a continuum from complete heterosexuality (total preference for the opposite sex) to complete homosexuality (total preference for the same sex), with most people falling primarily to one side or another and some falling in the middle (bi-sexual).

Whether a man is "feminine" or a woman is "masculine" in their appearance or body language does not mean the person is gay or lesbian. Some football players, construction workers, and muscle builders are gay. Some men who seem feminine are straight (heterosexual). Some gay men and lesbians have casual sex, and some are in committed relationships.

Sometimes people who were molested by someone of the same sex and were sexually aroused by it worry that they may be gay. They worry because they see that gay people are often treated badly by others, or because their religion says that homosexuality is wrong. Being molested does not "cause" homosexuality. *Most* people can be aroused by persons of the same sex as well as by someone of the opposite sex. Many straight people have had sexual experiences with persons of the same sex. Most people experiment, finding out about their sexual preferences. If you molested a child of the same sex, it does not mean you are gay or lesbian. Most adult child molesters that we know of are heterosexual in their sexual relationships with other adults.

We are not telling you to approve or disapprove of same sex relationships between consenting peers. It is important, however, to recognize some of your thinking errors about about homosexuals, to respect other people's choices, and to apply your empathy skills to what they might be feeling.

EXERCISE 48. HOMOSEXUALITY

1) **Personal questions:**

Is there someone in your family or someone you know who identifies as gay or lesbian? ______________

If so, who? ____

How do you feel about that person or persons? ______________________________

____

How do you feel when he/she visits and your friends are around?______________________

What do you think that person may have felt when people make fun of homosexuals?______________

Have you ever had questions about your own sexual preferences? ____________________

If so, what have you wondered about and why? ______________________________

____

Have you had any experiences with gays or lesbians? If so, what were some of these experiences? ________

____

____

2) **General questions:**

What is your opinion about homosexuality? (Okay, weird, don't care, interested, grossed out, or ?) _______

____

____

What is the basis for your opinion? (What was said by parents, religion, other literature, friends, or experiences

____

____

3) **Situations:** Read these situations, then answer the questions that follow.

a) Joe is 16 years old. He is captain of the football team, a good student and well-liked at school. He comes from an ordinary family. Ever since he was a little kid, he always felt a little different from his friends. When he turned 13, he realized that while his friends began to have romantic thoughts about girls, he had fantasies about boys. He didn't tell anyone. When all his friends dated girls, he did too. When he was 15, he picked Penny as his girlfriend primarily because it was easy to talk to her. He kissed her and felt her breasts and went as far as she would let him, just like his friends did with their girlfriends. But it didn't turn him on. He was much more attracted to his best friend Pete. Joe realized he was gay. Pete was heterosexual, so Joe never told him how he felt. He hid his sexuality. Sometimes the other guys told jokes about gays. He laughed with the rest of them. When they called guys they didn't like "faggots," he never said anything. He hid what he was feeling.

How do you think Joe felt when his friends called people "faggots"? ____________________

____

____

How do you think Joe felt when his friends told jokes about gays? ____________________

____

____

Why do you think he laughed when they did? ______________________________

____

Why do you think Joe never told his friend Pete how he felt? ______________________________

____

Why do you think Joe went out with Penny and was sexual with her? ______________________________

____

Why do you think Joe hid his true sexuality? ______________________________

____

____

b) Paul's parents were divorced when he was 7 years old. He didn't see much of his father. When Paul was 9, his teacher, Mr. Andrews, befriended him. He talked to Paul and took him camping. On many of the camping trips, Mr. Andrews molested Paul. He masturbated Paul and had Paul masturbate him. When Mr. Andrews masturbated him, Paul felt very sexually excited. Mr. Andrews told Paul that Paul was a homosexual because Paul was aroused by the masturbation. When Paul completed the fourth grade, he did not see Mr. Andrews any more. Paul felt relieved, because he felt funny about what had happened. When Paul was a teenager, he was attracted to girls in his class, but he felt afraid to ask any out, because of what Mr. Andrews had told him about being homosexual.

Do you think Paul is a homosexual? ____________ Why or why not? ______________________________

____

Do you think Mr. Andrews is a homosexual? ____________ Why or why not? ______________________________

____

Why was Paul aroused by the masturbation? Why did Paul keep going camping with Mr. Andrews after he was molested the first time? ______________________________

____

If Paul was gay, was it still molestation? ____________ Why or why not? ______________________________

____

____

SEX AND SEX OFFENDING

As we said before, sex offending is misusing sex to meet your own needs for power or intimacy, to express anger, or to relieve tension and boredom, with someone who doesn't understand and can't or doesn't legally consent.

Some sex offenders are more attracted to children than they are to people of the same or similar age. *There are laws in all states prohibiting sex with children.* Children are not legally capable of consenting. They are easily overpowered by someone older or stronger or in a position of authority.

If you are attracted to children and allow yourself to have sexual thoughts or fantasies about them, you are placing yourself in a position of danger. You are on the third step of the offense chain. It is important that you learn to turn off these thoughts. Tell your therapist about them, and get help to retrain your sexual urges toward someone capable of consenting. In fact, *any time you have a sexual thought that can get you into trouble, it is important to stop and change that thought.*

Earlier in the book, we talked about yelling "stop" to yourself and/or replacing dangerous fantasies with fantasies of something unpleasant as a way of stopping the fantasies. These unpleasant fantasies can include things you find embarrassing, repulsive, or fearful. Unpleasant fantasies can include things that might happen during or after the illegal sexual behavior, like someone you respect walking in on you while you are molesting, or thoughts of being arrested at school.

Because we're talking about the sexual part of sex offending, the exercise below gives you an opportunity to review what you've learned about Urge Control (Chapter Six). Before you do Exercise 49, it is important to get instructions from your counselor or therapist on how best to work with your dangerous fantasies.

EXERCISE 49. REPLACING DANGEROUS FANTASIES

1) In replacing dangerous fantasies with unpleasant ones, you can use your senses of sight, taste, hearing, and touch. Think of three unpleasant fantasies of each type. (For example, for sight your example could be something that grosses you out, like looking at your insides coming out after being cut with a knife.) Make them as awful as you can.

a) Unpleasant *sight* fantasies:

1) ______________________________

2) ______________________________

3) ______________________________

b) Unpleasant *taste* fantasies:

1) ______________________________

2) ______________________________

3) ______________________________

c) Unpleasant *hearing* fantasies:

1) ______________________________

2) ______________________________

3) ______________________________

d) Unpleasant *touch* fantasies:

1) ______________________________

2) ______________________________

3) ______________________________

2) Unpleasant fantasies can also be those that cause you to have an unpleasant emotion, like embarrassment or shame, terror or fear, or repulsion or disgust. They can consist of any object, person or group of people, animals or imaginary creatures, or any kind of experience. Let your imagination go wild. They can either be related to a potential offense or entirely unrelated. In this section of the exercise, think of three of the most awful fantasies you can that might cause you to feel embarrassed, terrified, or repulsed.

a) *Embarrassment* fantasies:

1) ____

2) ____

3) ____

b) *Terror* fantasies:

1) ____

2) ____

3) ____

c) *Repulsive* fantasies:

1) ____

2) ____

3) ____

3) Pick two or three of the most powerful of these unpleasant fantasies and write them down on a piece of paper. Every night next week after you go to bed, allow yourself to start having an improper fantasy. Yell "STOP" to yourself after no more than 10 seconds or before your fantasy gets to offending behavior. Then read and focus your mind on one of your two or three *awful* fantasies. Really get into it. Feel the awful feelings or sensory experiences. After the first week, you will need to practice this at least once a week. Any time you catch yourself in an inappropriate sexual fantasy, repeat the same process. If the unpleasant fantasy doesn't seem to be working, try another one, until you find some that do work.

You can also replace dangerous or deviant fantasies with warm, loving, sexual fantasies of mutually consenting sex with a person of your same or similar age. Developing relationships with appropriate persons of the same or similar age is an important way of changing deviant sexual fantasies. The way to begin a relationship is through friendship.

FRIENDSHIP

Friendship is defined in the dictionary as "the attachment of one person to another by feelings of affection or personal regard." We talk about friendship as a part of relapse prevention for various reasons. First, if you have close friends, you are less likely to isolate yourself, have inappropriate sexual fantasies, and make poor judgments that lead you down the *Offense Chain*. Second, if you find you are fantasizing or feel badly about yourself and your life, you will have someone you can call and talk to about your thoughts and feelings instead of offending. Finally, if you understand the difference between friendship and love and sex, you are less likely to inappropriately mix up sex with the friendship of a young child or a friend who doesn't want a sexual relationship.

A *relationship* is a connection or involvement with another person. We often talk about relationships as a love connection, although it can be a simple friendship. Love relationships should develop gradually, in a way where trust can gradually build, starting with a very casual acquaintanceship, and building into closer and closer friendship. Once you have a very close friendship, you may want to move further into the area of love and sexual intimacy. If you move into love and sexual intimacy without a solid foundation of friendship, you are more likely to be hurt, or have your trust betrayed.

The diagram below shows how relationships should build.

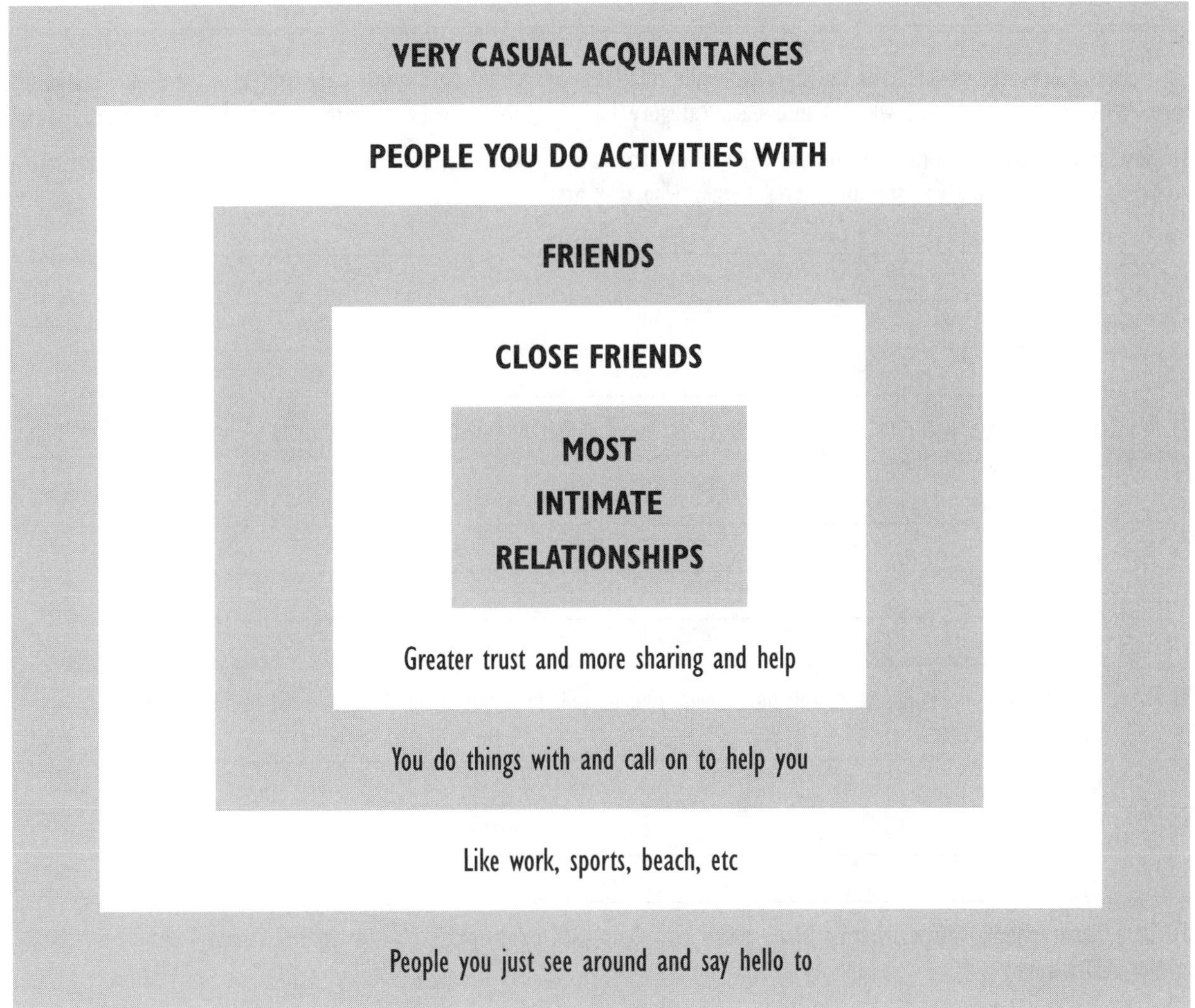

Note that at each level as you move inward, you should be able to trust and depend on the other person more and more. If the person seriously lets you down at one level, you can just move him/her outward to the next ring, perhaps temporarily, until you work through your differences and trust builds again between you. You don't have to dump this friend entirely, because you know this person can be trusted or depended on at a less intimate level – for some things, but not for others.

Often people, especially abuse victims who have difficulty with boundaries, meet a person and immediately take him or her into the innermost level, sharing their most intimate thoughts and feelings before they have any way to determine if the person is trustworthy. If the person breaks their trust at that level, they feel that they have to throw the person out of *all* the relationship circles, because there is no trust or connection on any other level to fall back on. This is a kind of "black and white" thinking, as if a person is either perfect or rotten, with nothing in between. It's much better to have a solid friendship first that becomes closer and closer, and then winds up at the right level of comfort. You will have choices to move in closer or push the relationship out further. It does not have to be an all-or-none situation.

EXERCISE 50. LEVELS OF FRIENDSHIP CLOSENESS

In this exercise, we will take the steps from the relationship diagram on the last page and turn them into categories here. Write down the people who fit into each category for you. (You may have more or less than the space allows.)

1) *Very casual acquaintances* (people you say hello to or chat casually with, but don't actually do anything with or invite home) – describe where you see them, or generally who they are:

a) ______________________________

b) ______________________________

c) ______________________________

d) ______________________________

2) *People you do activities with* (like sports, or music, or working, but not much more than that) – list them by first name and say what you do with them:

a) ______________________________

b) ______________________________

c) ______________________________

d) ______________________________

3) *Friends* (people you do things with, call on to help you, or talk to about some things) – list by first name:

a) ______________________________

b) ______________________________

c) ______________________________

d) ______________________________

4) *Close friends* (people you really trust, share more with, help each other, plus all of the former items) – list by first name and/or relationship:

a) ______________________________

b) ______________________________

c) ______________________________

5) *Most intimate relationship(s)* (the one or more persons you most trust, share with, and feel closest to in the world: your best friend[s]) – list by first name and/or relationship:

a) ______________________________

b) ______________________________

There are likely to be fewer people in each category as the relationship or friendship becomes closer and more intimate. Notice that your most intimate relationship may be with your brother or your mother and does not include sex. Sex is a separate element you may or may not have at whatever level you decide. If you and the other person who decide to have sex are at the most intimate relationship level, it tends to increase the intimacy of the relationship.

The role of *touch* in a relationship is important. You are most likely here because you *inappropriately* touched someone you knew. There are many different types and levels of touch, from a simple handshake to a punch or pat, to hugging and kissing, to more explicitly sexual touches. Just like friendships, touch is on a scale from casual to intimate. Nonsexual touching includes holding hands, putting an arm on someone's shoulder, patting someone's arm or back, giving hugs, pulling hair, and hitting (not all nonsexual touch is good touch). Sexual touching includes romantic kissing and touching, touching any private areas of the body, rubbing private parts against somebody, as well as oral sex, intercourse, and so forth.

It is important to know when to touch and when not to touch and when a particular type of touch is appropriate. If you don't know a person, you should not touch him/her. For example, it is *not* appropriate to touch a waitress or waiter in a restaurant. While it generally is appropriate to shake hands with someone you meet or to hug a good friend, it is also necessary to respect what the person you are about to touch wants. Some people like pats and hugs; others may not like to be touched at all. You have to listen, read body language (looks and movements), and not be afraid to ask what the other person would like. (This is also true in sexual touching.)

People will give you signals. You can usually tell if a person wants you to come closer by how they move toward you, face you, and look directly into your eyes. If they are not interested in you, they will usually look and move away. Ask if you are in doubt.

And take notice – sexual touching of a child under any circumstances is strictly forbidden under the law. Even though a child may seem to crave sexual touches, ***you are responsible not to sexually touch a child.*** The child probably is asking for affection and care, but has been molested and doesn't know how to get what he/she needs without submitting to sexual touches.

If you have molested a child, you should not be alone around children. Even with adults present, you should never put yourself in a position to reoffend or where you might be accused of improper touching.

The final exercise of this chapter is on appropriate touching.

EXERCISE 51. TOUCHING

1) For the following situations, tell if the touching was proper or improper and why.

a) Julio had breakfast at a Denny's Restaurant. The waitress was very nice to him. He gave her a hug as he was leaving. Proper or improper? ____________ Why? ____

____

____

b) Matt was introduced to Mary. He shook her hand. Proper or improper? ____________ Why? ____________

____

____

c) Jane saw an old friend who had moved away. She ran over and hugged her. Proper or improper? ______Why?

____

____

d) Al was talking with his friends. A girl walked by. Al patted her on the butt. Proper or improper?_______Why?

____

____

e) Lisa complained that her shoulder was sore. Roger, a casual friend, offered to massage it. Lisa said, "Sure, okay," so he did. Proper or improper? ___________ Why? ___________

f) As Roger was massaging Lisa's shoulder, he moved his hand down to her chest. Proper or improper? ___________ Why? ___________

g) Tony ran into his old friend Dave at the mall. They hadn't seen each other for weeks. Tony gave Dave a light punch in the shoulder. Proper or improper? ___________ Why? ___________

h) Sally saw a little child all alone, looking sad, in the park. She didn't know the child, but she picked her up and hugged and kissed her and told her she would be okay. Proper or improper? ___________ Why? ___________

i) Tony's little cousin ran to him in the park and jumped into his arms. Tony gave him a big hug and then put him down. Proper or improper? ___________ Why? ___________

j) After Tom took Anna to the movies and for pizza, they drove to her house. Anna sat on the far edge of the seat, away from Tom, talking but not looking directly at Tom. When they got to the house Tom pulled Anna to him and kissed her. Proper or improper? ___________ Why? ___________

k) Jack was at a party. A girl he had never met stared at him and began to move toward him. He went over to her. They talked intently. He put his arm around her shoulder. Proper or improper? ___________ Why? ___________

l) Jack walked the girl outside. She continued to talk to him, looking him in the eye, and stood very close. He gave her a romantic kiss. Proper or improper? ___________ Why? ___________

m) If Jack and the girl had walked outside for air, but she stood well away from him, and kept looking around for her other friends, and Jack grabbed her and gave her a romantic kiss, would it have been proper or improper? ___________ Why? ___________

n) Joe was on a packed bus. He accidentally rubbed against a young woman standing next to him. She didn't say anything, so he deliberately rubbed against her another time. Proper or improper? ___________ Why? ___________

o) 10-year-old Tina had been molested by her step-father when she was little. She lived in a series of foster homes afterward. Abe was babysitting for her. He was sitting on the sofa and watching TV. Tina came up and sat on his lap with her legs rubbing against his penis and hugged him. He hugged her back, allowing her legs to continue to rub against his penis. Proper or improper? ____________ Why? ____

____

p) Chad's little cousin had been molested by a teacher. Chad wouldn't let her sit on his lap. He would only give her a hug in front of her mother, and then only a quick hug. Proper or improper? ____________ Why? ____________

____

q) Josh met a Ellen at a party. He enjoyed talking to her, but was not interested in being sexual or intimately involved with her. She kept coming closer to him, putting her arms around his shoulders, and brushing her lips on his cheek. He kept moving and looking away. Were her actions proper or improper? __________ Why? ______________

____

2) Now is the time for your experiences. Tell of a time you touched someone properly and of a time you touched someone improperly and why.

a) Properly: ____

____

Why was your action proper? ____

____

b) Improperly: ____

____

Why was your action improper? ____

____

Remember, you too have a right not to be touched at any time or in a way you don't want to be touched. Touch is situational and personal. Know when is an appropriate time to touch a person in a specific way and then whether or not the person wishes to be touched. Know when and how *you* want or don't want to be touched. And especially be careful when and how you touch children.

SUMMARY

What you have covered in this chapter:

1) That sex, love and friendship are three different things
2) Different ways sex is misused
3) What you want in a love relationship
4) What turns you on sexually
5) Some information about homosexuality
6) How to replace dangerous sexual fantasies
7) The importance of friendship
8) The different levels of friendship and/or relationships
9) About appropriate and inappropriate touching

NOTES

CHAPTER TWELVE

FOR FAMILIES

Now is your opportunity to work together with your family, to share with them what you have learned about your offense chain and to practice your communication skills with them. It is important that you and your therapist schedule meetings to work together with your family. It is important for the members of your family with whom you now live, or will when you return home, to participate. Any additional family members are optional. Since they will be expected to do the exercises, you will need to make extra copies of some of the pages and exercises from this chapter for them.

Sharing your new knowledge is an important way to help your family to learn about offense behavior, to rebuild trust, and to help you with your relapse prevention program. It will also serve as a review of what we have covered in this workbook.

Families often have a hard time communicating, especially when one family member has sexually offended, and even more when the victim is also a family member. To help communication happen safely, these exercises should be done in a family session with your therapist. You will be doing the exercises along with the other members of your family.

If you sexually abused a brother or sister, you should have had joint therapy with that sibling to clarify issues for the victim *before* you sit down with the whole family to do this work. This work should be done *only* when the victim's therapist has agreed he/she is ready.

From now on, in the exercises, instructions to you offenders will be in italics, like this – *Tell your family*. . . Instructions to the rest of the family will be in regular type.

EXERCISE 52. BASICS OF RELAPSE PREVENTION

Part I. The Offense Chain

Make a big poster of your offense chain, showing the ***SUD, Dangerous Situation, Lapse, Giving up,*** *and* ***Offense*** *behavior. Talk through your offense chain. Explain each step of your actions, how you were feeling, and what you told yourself (were thinking) at each step. You can use your offense chains from Exercise Numbers 1 and 20 to refresh your memory.*

You will be helping your family to understand that behavior has many steps and that thoughts and feelings influence behavior. One of the best ways to learn is by doing, so they will break down their behavior into its steps, just as you broke down your offense into its steps on the offense chain. Even though they will be using the same process and the same language, this does ***not*** *mean that the behavior they describe is as serious or illegal as your sexual offending.*

Now it the family's turn. Each of you can do this. Help younger children who may have difficulty. They can do it too. Looking at the steps of an *Offense Chain,* apply them to something you did that you felt sorry about afterward. It is best to pick a behavior you have done more than once or fear repeating. For little kids, this can include misbehaviors at school such as being tardy, talking back to a teacher, stealing, getting into a fight, forgetting homework, or not doing it, and so forth. For teens and adults, it might include spending too much money on something, getting drunk, over-eating, blowing up at or being impatient with family members, etc. Think of a specific time you did this. Once you have decided on the problem behavior and situation, take it apart and see what led up to it following the *Offense Chain* format. (Sometimes it is easier to start from the problem behavior and work backwards.)

The following is an example of an actual chain made by the 5-year-old sister of an offender. She had gotten into trouble several times at school for chewing gum.

1) **Seemingly Unimportant Decision (SUD)** (what started the whole chain – it is the seemingly innocent choice she made that put her in the "zone of danger"): *taking gum to school so she could chew it afterward at her friend's house.*

2) **Dangerous Situation** (this is a spot where she had the opportunity to do the problem behavior): *being in the classroom with gum in her pocket.*

3) **Lapse** (this is either where she began to daydream or think about the problem behavior or did something that placed her much closer to doing the problem act): *taking the gum out just to smell it, and thinking about how sweet it would taste.*

4) **Giving Up** (almost doing the act, feeling like she has already crossed the line and there is no turning back): *touching her tongue to the gum and figuring she already broke the rule so she may as well put it in her mouth.*

5) **Problem Behavior:** *chewing gum in class.*

Now, using the same format, each of you look at your own problem behavior.

1) **Seemingly Unimportant Decision (SUD)** (what started the whole chain? – it is the seemingly innocent choice you made which put you in the "zone of danger"): ____________________

____

2) **Dangerous Situation** (this is the spot where you had the opportunity to do the problem behavior):

____

3) **Lapse** (this is either where you began to think about doing the behavior or did some act that was dangerously close to the problem behavior): Thought or fantasy ____________________

____

Act____

____

4) **Giving Up** (this is the spot where you figure you've already failed and may as well continue): ______

____

____

5) **Problem Behavior** ____________________________

____

The purpose of doing this chain is to learn about the steps of any behavior. Once we become aware of each step, we can change the direction, so the negative result will not happen. At each step in the chain, behavior can be changed to avoid the negative result. The earlier in the chain a safe alternative decision is made, the safer the person is from reoffending. You can help your offending family member by reminding him/her of the *choices* available at each step.

In the case of the gum-chewing student, if she had not brought the gum to school at all, she would not have been able to break the rule. Once she had the gum at school, however, she could have asked the teacher to hold it for her until the end of school, so it would be out of her reach. If she failed to do that, she could have given it to a friend to hold once she was fantasizing about chewing it and had taken a smell of it. And once her tongue touched it, she could still have thrown it away. Each of these actions would have protected her from doing the problem behavior.

She could also have changed her thinking at each step. In the morning before school, she could have thought, "I can miss my gum for one day. It isn't worth being tempted at school." Once she had the gum at school, she could have thought, "I better find some way to protect myself from temptation. Maybe I'd better put my gum somewhere where I can't get at it." Once she began to daydream about it and unwrapped it, she could have thought, "I'd better get rid of this fast or I'll begin to chew it, and I don't want to get in trouble again." And at the giving up point where she actually put her tongue on it, she could have said to herself, "It's not too late. I can still stop myself by throwing it away."

Part II. Alternative Behaviors and Thoughts

Now it is your turn to explain what you could have done instead at each step of your offense chain. Also explain what you could say to yourself at the same time, that would help you make the correct choices. Remember to use ***Avoidance*** *and* ***Escape****.*

Family members: List the other behaviors and different thinking each of you could use to avoid your problem behaviors. Use the situation you described in Part I.

1) At the **Seemingly Unimportant Decision (SUD)** stage:

Different thought: ______________________________

Other behavior: ______________________________

2) At the **Dangerous Situation** stage:

Different thought: ______________________________

Other behavior: ______________________________

3) At the **Lapse** stage:

Different thought: ______________________________

Other behavior: ______________________________

4) At the **Giving Up** stage:

Different thought: ______________________________

Other behavior: ______________________________

Part III. Working on Family Issues

The most difficult part of this exercise is to apply this *Offense Chain* and *Relapse Prevention* model to find ways to change some situations or patterns at home in order to help the offender stop his/her offending behavior. While the offender is 100% responsible for his/her own actions, there may be other factors that could have influenced his behavior, and, if changed, can have a positive impact in the future. It is the awareness of these factors that can help the family help the offender. The family and offender can work together as a team to prevent reoffense. (You can either do this part of the exercise individually or as a group or groups, such as parents together, children together, or by females, males, or in age groupings, depending on how many of you there are.)

Think of what problems might have been (or positive things that weren't) going on in the family shortly before your adolescent family member sexually offended. How well were you communicating with each other? How often did the whole family spend time together? When one of you was having a problem or made a mistake, could you go to the family for help? What was the family's reaction when you did have a problem? How strict was the discipline in your family? How were the rules made? What happened when a rule was broken by a child? By an adult? Did you feel respected by the other family members, including both children and adults? What kinds of behaviors showed that respect? What was your work or school schedule like? Did you take time to have fun together? How often was alcohol used by family members? How often were tranquilizers or other mood-altering drugs (including prescription and street drugs) used by a family member? Did one family member get a lot more attention than the others? Did everyone have some privacy as well as time together? What happened when you expressed your feelings? What other issues were going on in the family? Talk about the answers to these questions with the therapist who is helping with these family sessions.

Write down a problem in your family using the *Offense Chain* format. Then write down things you could do to change the situation at various points in the chain. This format provides you with a way to catch problems early and head them off, or, if they have developed already, to change them. For example, if the family problem was communication, you could look at it like this:

1) **SUD**: Everyone is busy with his/her own life and problems.
2) **Dangerous Situation**: Communication may break again down if something isn't done about the situation.
3) **Lapse**: Nobody has had time to stop and talk or listen for the past week.
4) **Giving Up**: You figure since nobody wants to talk to you, you won't talk with anybody, either.
5) **Problem**: Family members don't communicate.

Now let us look at what one child could do about the problem at one or more of the steps along the way:

1) Request a family meeting to talk about communication.
2) Sit down with a parent or with brothers and/or sisters and discuss the issue.
3) Get together with brothers and sisters and make a plan to help family members communicate.
4) Get someone to be an ally, to help approach others in the family.
5) Write a letter to parents and/or kids who aren't talking about issues and problems.
6) Make sure that he/she is openly asserting his/her communication needs.
7) Present the family members with a taped message requesting improved communication.
8) Call a therapist, counselor, other relative, or minister and request help.
9) If the situation seems hopeless, find someone outside of the home to talk to.

Use the same process for *your* family issue or problem, filling in the spaces below:

1) **SUD** (What is the family or one or more members choosing to do that may put it in a dangerous situation?) ____________________

____

2) **Dangerous Situation** (What negative or dangerous thing could now happen?) ____________________

____

____

3) **Lapse** (What is the first step toward the serious family problem that might occur?) ____________________

____

____

4) **Giving Up** ____________________

____

____

5) **Problem** ____________________

____

____

What could you do about this problem and at each step leading to it? Remember, the sooner you do something, the less serious the problem will be. List *at least* 5 solutions.

1) ______________________________
2) ______________________________
3) ______________________________
4) ______________________________
5) ______________________________
6) ______________________________
7) ______________________________
8) ______________________________
9) ______________________________
10) ______________________________

The important thing to be aware of in all situations is that you all have choices. The choices are not always exactly what you want them to be. For example, you may not be able to get your family to be very communicative. But you have the choice of finding others to talk with, or of talking with one or more members of the family who are available, or of writing your feelings instead. The point is that everyone has choices.

When you see a problem beginning to arise and know it may affect the family member who has acted out sexually, it is important to either talk to that person or get a parent to talk to him/her, be there for him/her as needed, or suggest some alternatives. It's not your job to rescue someone else in your family. Each family member is responsible for his/her own behavior. But a little support can go a long way.

The most important change you can make is for each family member to communicate his or her feelings and needs. *Communication is at the cornerstone of a healthy family structure.* Even if family members cannot do anything about another person's feelings and needs, just listening to the other person can make that person feel understood and appreciated.

When someone is in pain, particularly, most of us want to help that person out of the pain. While it may be possible to make some kinds of emotional pain go away for a young child, older children and adults must handle the pain themselves. Instead of saying to them, "It could be worse," "That's nothing compared to what happened to me," "Don't think about it," or attempting to solve the problem for them, it is more helpful to listen and just be there for them. That gives them the strength and self-esteem to find their own solutions.

Sometimes families live together, do work and recreational activities together, but forget to talk to each other about what they think, feel, and need. They believe that since the family knows its members so well, they automatically know what you are feeling or needing. It is easy to feel ignored or abandoned when no one responds to what you think are clear signals.

The next exercise encourages communication on some touchy issues. You are going to need lots of extra paper, because each of you will be called upon to write something to every other family member, and you will need to duplicate what you write for each family member. This exercise should be done in a family session with the adolescent offender's therapist.

EXERCISE 53. FAMILY COMMUNICATION

1) **Family Appreciation:** Write down on separate pieces of paper what you really appreciate about each family member. In a family meeting, read what you have written out loud, then give the family members their papers. After everyone is done, each family member shares how these comments made him/her feel.

2) **Family Problems:** Write down on separate pieces of paper what bothers you most in the behavior of each family member. Be specific. (This can include things like "not listening to me," "bossing me around," "expecting too much of me," "drinking too much," "not doing chores," and so forth). Be brave! Next to each item, write what you would like that person to do or be like instead. Each writer will read the things that bother him/her, what he/she wants from that family member, then have the family member tell how the comments made him/her feel. The family member is not allowed to argue about what was written or get back at the person who wrote it, but just talk about how it made him/her feel.

3) **Communicating Offense, Offender and Victim Feelings:** Fill out your responses, then discuss and explain your answers in the family group. *(To help with this exercise, make copies of the feeling list from Chapter Four for your family.)*

a) What are your feelings about the sex offense that was committed by your son, daughter, sister, or brother? Write your feelings down here. (If there was more than one offense in the family, write about each or about sex offenses in general.) *(The offender writes about his/her own feelings about the offense.)* ______________

____

____

____

____

____

____

b) What do you feel about the offender? *(The offender writes what he/she feels about him/herself.)*______________

____

____

____

____

____

c) What do you think the victim must be feeling about the offense and him/herself? (If you have trouble with this, try to imagine yourself in the victim's shoes. Pretend you have just had the offense happen to you, or think of a time you had a similar experience. How would you have felt, or did you feel?)______________

____

____

____

____

____

____

4) **Becoming More Aware of Communication:** Each family member should answer the following questions, then discuss them in a family session.

a) Think of a time when someone in your family really **listened to you.**

1) Who listened to you? ______________________________

2) What were you talking about? ______________________________

3) Where were both of you at the time? ______________________________

4) Did the other person stand or sit? ____________ How close? ______________

5) Did the person look at you all the time? ______________________________

6) How was the person acting? ______________________________

7) What made it easy to talk to the person? ______________________________

8) What did that person say to you (how did he/she respond)? ______________

9) How did it feel to be listened to? ______________________________

____

b) Now think of a time when **you really listened** to a family member.

1) Who was that family member ______________________________

2) What was he/she talking about? ______________________________

3) Where were both of you at the time? ______________________________

4) What were you feeling at the time (why did you want to listen?) ______________

____

5) How was the other person acting? ______________________________

____

6) Did the other person stand or sit? ____________ How close? ______________

7) Did the person look at you all the time? ______________________________

8) How loud or soft was the person's voice? ______________________________

9) What else made it easier for you to listen? ______________________________

____

5) **Improving Communication**:

a) What steps can you take to make it easier for other family members to **listen** to you?

1) ____

2) ____

3) ____

4) ____

b) What steps can you take to make it easier for the family members to **talk** to you?

1) ____

2) ____

3) ____

4) ____

c) What are some ways the family as a whole could improve communication?

1) ____

2) ____

3) ____

4) ____

Discuss the ways each family member listed in part 5 and decide on four specific things the family will do together to improve communication and four specific things each of you will do individually. Also think of a way to get the family together to reactivate these plans if the family begins to slip back into poor communication. Write all of these down on a piece of paper and post them on a bulletin board, the refrigerator, or somewhere else where you all will see them. And add the reminder, in large letters: "We will take time to listen to each other. " The results will be well worth the effort.

Often, in families where an adolescent commits a sex offense, there has been prior sexual or other abuse of the offender and of other family members. Some or all of the family members may have been victims. For example, 13-year-old Randy, who had molested his 5-year-old sister, eventually revealed that his 16-year-old brother had masturbated him when he was 9 or 10 years old. This was a molestation. When the 16-year-old brother was questioned, he revealed that he had only done what was done to him. He had been molested by some older boys on the block. As we talked about this with the whole family, Randy's 19-year-old brother said he had been molested by his uncle. Randy's mother divulged that she had been molested as a child by her uncle and cousin and raped by a stranger, and Randy's father admitted he had been molested by his older brother.

Even though these assaults happened in the past, it is important to talk about them openly. When victimizations have been put aside without talking through your thoughts and feelings about them, the feelings are held down. This prevents the victim from being able to feel these emotions in other situations or to understand what others may be feeling. It causes the victimized person to shut down and be emotionally distant from spouses, brothers and sisters, or children. When these emotions are not felt and shown appropriately, some victims act out their feelings in ways such as drug and alcohol abuse, violence, and so forth. Have you ever punched some one or hit the wall or slammed a door instead of saying, "I'm angry with you about..." This is an example of acting out feelings instead of talking them through.

In Randy's family, once the family members were able to talk about what had happened to them and about all of the embarrassment, shame, helplessness, anger, guilt, and even pleasure that they had felt, they were more open to how the other family members were feeling. Just revealing what had happened to each other and cleaning out these old wounds by dredging up old, buried emotions, improved their relationships with each other a lot. It helped them understand why they may have done ineffective, hurtful, or self-destructive things. People react to other people or events with hurtful behavior when they don't know how to talk about their feelings. Talking about their victimizations especially improved their understanding of their youngest son's sex offense.

The next exercise is your opportunity to look at your own victimization. All of us have experienced some type of sexual, physical, or emotional victimization in our lives. These experiences could have happened within the family or outside of it, and could also include such things as being beaten up at school, discriminated against by a teacher, robbed, treated unfairly, or let down by a friend. If you have been victimized a lot, pick three of the most severe and significant times. If you have a lot of feelings, bad dreams, or are getting upset a lot in talking about victimization, you might need the help of a therapist for a while to work through your feelings. Ask the therapist who is working with the offender for a referral if you do not have a therapist of your own.

EXERCISE 54. PROCESSING VICTIMIZATIONS

1) Think back to some times in your life when you were victimized. Write down what happened and how you felt.

a) What occurred:____

How you felt afterward: ____

b) What occurred:____

How you felt afterward: ____

c) What occurred:____

How you felt afterward:

2) In writing below, tell your perpetrator (of each victimization) what you feel about what he/she did to you and what you feel about that person.

a) ____

b) ______________________________

____

____

____

____

c) ______________________________

____

____

____

____

3) Think about how you felt when you were a victim, then write a brief letter to the victim of the adolescent offender in your family, telling the person that you understand how he/she might feel, and expressing emotional support and your regret for what the offender did. (*The offender can write the same letter, expressing his/her own regret.*)

Dear ______________________________ ,

____

Signed: ______________________________

Expressing Family Love and Affection: Humans thrive on expressions of affection. These can be verbal (such as telling someone you care about him/her), nonverbal (such as doing things for the person like attending their ball games, giving flowers, or baking cookies, or just being there for him/her), or physical (like hugging, kissing, or patting, or putting a hand on another person's shoulder.

Appropriate physical contact, in particular, is necessary for babies to thrive, and it is still needed by most adults. Yet, often, in our modern world, people get so busy or distracted that they forget to give a simple pat or hug.

Since the family can and should be the most important place to get appropriate affection, it is important to look at how your family functions in this regard. The next short exercise is designed to help you look at your family's ways of expressing affection, and encourage healthy demonstrations of love and caring. Each family member should do the exercise, then everyone should discuss the responses.

EXERCISE 55. SHOWING AFFECTION

1) How often have you expressed your affection toward your family members in the following ways?

TYPE OF AFFECTION	APPROXIMATE NUMBER OF TIMES DONE LAST WEEK
a) Hugged....................................	______________________
b) Kissed....................................	______________________
c) Patted....................................	______________________
d) Put your hand on person..........	______________________
e) Put your arm around shoulder.	______________________
f) (Other physical).........................	______________________
g) Done something special for.......	______________________
h) Given a gift to..........................	(what?)__________________
i) Made something for..................	(what?)__________________
j) Gone out of your way for..........	______________________
k) Told the person you cared.........	______________________
l) Said how important he/she was	______________________
m) Took an interest in and listened to	______________________
n) (Other)......................................	______________________

2) How often have persons in your family done these things with you in the past week?

TYPE OF AFFECTION	APPROXIMATE NUMBER OF TIMES DONE LAST WEEK
a) Hugged....................................	______________________
b) Kissed....................................	______________________
c) Patted....................................	______________________
d) Put your hand on person..........	______________________

TYPE OF AFFECTION	APPROXIMATE NUMBER OF TIMES DONE LAST WEEK
e) Put your arm around shoulder.	______
f) (Other physical)	______
g) Done something special for	______
h) Given a gift to	(what?) ______
i) Made something for	(what?) ______
j) Gone out of your way for	______
k) Told the person you cared.........	______
l) Said how important he/she was	______
m) Took an interest in and listened to	______
n) (Other)	______

3) For the next week, record how many times you do each of the following things. Try to do at least one of each for each member of the family, with the exception of g), h), i)or j), which do not need to be done quite as frequently.

TYPE OF AFFECTION	TIMES DONE THIS WEEK
a) Hugged	______
b) Kissed	______
c) Patted	______
d) Put your hand on person	______
e) Put your arm around shoulder.	______
f) (Other physical)	______
g) Done something special for	______
h) Given a gift to	(what?) ______
i) Made something for	(what?) ______
j) Gone out of your way for	______
k) Told the person you cared.........	______
l) Said how important he/she was	______
m) Took an interest in and listened to	______
n) (Other)	______

Do what is comfortable, but if you seem not to be expressing affection, make an extra effort to show your affection appropriately. If everyone in the family tries to express their affection regularly in a variety of ways, family members will probably be happier with each other.

Inappropriate affection is physical contact that violates personal boundaries. Personal boundaries are limits that protect a person from harm. Body privacy is one of these personal boundaries. Every person is entitled to body privacy. Even babies are entitled to the privacy of not being poked, pinched, penetrated, or having their sexual parts fondled. Children should have privacy in the bathroom and while dressing. Even in play, nobody should grab a person's sexual parts.

Kisses should only occur between people who are very close and consenting. Children should never be forced to kiss anyone. Kisses between family members and with children should be totally non-sexual, not using tongues. They should not be placed on sexually arousing places, such as ears.

Sex offenders have broken through those personal boundaries when they committed their offenses. Consequently, boundary lines now must be even more firmly and clearly drawn. Families can help the offender not step over these boundaries. For example, it is *not* okay for the offender to take a little brother or sister to the bathroom at the mall while Mom is trying on clothes. Mom should not ask the offender to do this. If the offender takes a little brother or sister to the bathroom, the offender's boundaries are critically weakened. The offender will be making a *SUD (Seemingly Unimportant Decision)* by agreeing, and it will place him or her in a *Dangerous Situation* on the *Offense Chain.* It is important for family members not to ask the offender to do anything that will place him/her in a *Dangerous Situation.* Families as well as offenders must think ahead to the possible consequences of their requests and actions.

The following exercise can help the family see situations that could weaken the offender's boundaries and place the offender on the chain toward reoffense. It can help the offender reinforce his/her avoidance and escape responses. After each family member fills this out, discuss the answers in your therapy session.

EXERCISE 56. BOUNDARIES AND CONSEQUENCES

Part I. In the spaces following each of the following situations, write whether you think the offender's boundaries could be weakened and what the possible consequences could be if the offender agreed to do what was asked. *(On the space following the italicized line, the offender will write what he could say and do if faced with these situations.)*

1) Sandy had previously molested a nephew. Late one night, when Sandy's father was doing the dishes, he heard his 7-year-old son Don crying in bed. He turned to Sandy and said, "Go see what's troubling Don." Boundaries likely to be weakened or not? ______

Possible consequences? ______

If you were Sandy, what would you say and do? ______

______

2) Guillermo was previously arrested for exposing himself at night around the apartments where the family lived. Late one night, Guillermo's older brother said, "The garbage really smells. Guillermo, will you take it out?" Boundaries likely to be weakened or not? ______ Possible consequences? ______

If you were Guillermo, what would you say and do? ______

______

3) Yoko had previously molested her younger brother by fondling him. Late one night, her older brother said, "The garbage really smells. Yoko, will you take it out?" Boundaries likely to be weakened or not? Possible consequences? ______

If you were Yoko, what would you say and do? ______

______

How does this situation differ from the situation in number 2? ______

______

______

4) Tony had molested his little sister Carla several years ago. One morning before school, Carla called to him, "Tony, the zipper on my pants is caught. Will you come here and fix it for me?" Boundaries likely to be weakened or not?__________

Possible consequences? ____

____

What could Carla do instead? ____________________________________

____

If you were Tony, what would you say and do? ____________________________

____

5) Quazelle had been arrested for prowling (peeping in people's windows) at night. His mother came in with the groceries after work. As she was putting them away, she noticed that she had forgotten to buy bread, which she needed for the children's sandwiches in the morning. She had a splitting headache and wanted to go to bed, so she asked Quazelle, "Would you run over to the mini-mart and buy a loaf of bread?" Boundaries likely to be weakened or not? __________

Possible consequences? ____

____

If you were Quazelle, what would you say and do? __________________________

____

6) Yuri, a 17-year-old, was recently arrested for sex with a 12-year-old. Yuri's 12-year-old cousin Anna came for a visit. Yuri's grandmother wanted Anna to have a good time, so she said, "Yuri, take Anna to the show with you tonight." Boundaries likely to be weakened or not? __________ Possible consequences?____________________

____

*If you were Yuri, what would you say and do?*_____________________________

____

7) David had molested his little sister Sarah. Sarah was home with the chicken pox. Their mother had to go to work or she would lose her job, so she said, "David, I need you to stay home and babysit Sarah today. But make sure not to go into her room." Boundaries likely to be weakened or not? __________ Possible consequences?____________

____

____

*If you were David, what would you say and do?*____________________________

____

What could David's mother have done instead?____________________________

____

8) Lonnie had been arrested for molesting his brother Joey. The family was picnicking in the park. Lonnie's father said, "Lonnie and Joey, your job is to pick up the trash and put it in this bag, while I put away the rest of the food." Boundaries likely to be weakened or not? __________ Possible consequences?____________________

____

*What do you think about this example?*________________________________

____

____

____

____

Part II. Now it's time for each of you to brainstorm some situations that might actually happen in your family. These situations should be ones where you ask the offender to do something likely to weaken the offender's boundaries and result in his making a *SUD (Seemingly Unimportant Decision)* that could put him in a *Dangerous Situation.* Write down as many as you can as fast as you can. (Use another piece of paper if you think of more situations than the space allows.)

1) ____

____

2) ____

____

3) ____

____

4) ____

____

5) ____

____

6) ____

____

7) ____

____

8) ____

____

Now write: "I will not ask ____________________(fill in the offender's name) to:" above this list. Make a copy and keep it where you can look at it often.

Sex is often confused with affection and other emotions. While sex can be a demonstration of love and caring between two people, it also can be a simple physical gratification separate from any love and caring. Sex is also confused in our media with a wide variety of products, emotions, and images. Particularly when a young person has been previously sexually abused, sex gets confused with practically everything. The offending member of your family will do the next exercise alone, and then will share it with you.

EXERCISE 57. RELAPSE PREVENTION PLAN OUTLINE

With your therapist present, explain to your family how you mixed up sex with the expression of emotions and satisfaction of needs. Describe what was happening to you emotionally at the time of your offense and what needs you were trying to satisfy. Then tell your family how you will satisfy those needs in the future without offending again. Write down a plan to prevent relapse, sign it, and give a copy to your parents. Cover the topics on outline in the next exercise:

1) What I was feeling just before I committed my sex offense:

____

2) What I will do if I feel that way again (think of several things):

a) ____

b) ____

c) ____

d) ____

3) What I will do if I am asked to do something which is a ***SUD*** *(Seemingly Unimportant Decision) and could place me in a* ***Dangerous Situation*** *(think of several things):*

a) ____

b) ____

c) ____

d) ____

4) What I will do if I find myself in a ***Dangerous Situation*** *(think of several things):*

a) ____

b) ____

c) ____

d) ____

5) What I will do if I ***Lapse*** *in thoughts or behavior (think of several things):*

a) ____

b) ____

c) ____

d) ____

6) What I will do if I get to the ***Giving Up*** *stage (think of several things):*

a) ____

b) ____

c) ____

d) ____

7) Some of the alternative ways I will satisfy my needs:

a) ____

b) ____

c) ____

d) ____

8) *What I will do if communication breaks down in my family (think of several things):*

a) ____

b) ____

c) ____

d) ____

It is very important for parents, guardians, and other caretakers, no matter how busy, to listen whenever the offender comes to them with a problem related his/her *Relapse Prevention Plan*. For this reason, we ask them to enter into the following agreement. (Each parent, guardian, or other caretaker, signs a copy of this. Then post it in a place where it can be easily seen by the signer.)

EXERCISE 58. PARENTS' AGREEMENT

I am the (circle one) parent, guardian, or caretaker of (name of offender)

____.

I hereby agree to listen attentively to my offending child whenever he/she comes to me with a problem related to his/her Relapse Prevention Plan.

I will do my best to maintain healthy communication within our family, including going to our therapist or former therapist if needed.

Signed ______________________________ Dated ______________

Signed ______________________________ Dated ______________

Dealing with sexual offending behavior in a family is probably one of the hardest things you will do as a family. Many other issues will come up that you might need help in resolving. When that happens, don't be afraid to call your family therapist (if you have one, or ask the therapist who has been working with your offending family member to refer you to a family or individual therapist who has experience in working with families involved in sexual abuse).

It is also important that the family does not feel blamed for what the offender has done or will do. The offender is responsible for his/her own actions. The offender has the ability to choose what to do and what not to do. The family is a helper, to support and encourage the offender in making the most positive choices.

There are many additional topics you may think of and want to talk about, including roles, discipline, sexuality, other boundaries, re-uniting incest families, alcohol and other drugs, and so forth. This is just a selection. Add the additional topics that are important to you and your family. Expect that everyone's attitudes and beliefs may not be the same, but use this this as an important place for all of you to be able to clarify and reason out your values.

SUMMARY

You were able to increase your understanding of the following ideas in this chapter:

1) The basics of Relapse Prevention
2) Choices available to change destructive or self-destructive behavior
3) The importance of home support for the adolescent offender
4) The importance of good communication in the family
5) How victims feel
6) Appropriate ways of showing and increasing the expression of affection while respecting boundaries
7) The misuse of sexuality by adolescent offenders

ENDING THOUGHTS

Completing this workbook took a lot of time and effort, but it is time and effort well spent. You can congratulate yourself on a major accomplishment. But it is not enough just to read the material and do the exercises. You have to weave your learnings into your life and practice them every day. It is hard to break old habits, but, with practice, you can create new, positive habits to replace them. *Relapse Prevention*, in a nutshell, is a process you can use throughout your life.

You might want to check out how thoroughly you absorbed the material. In the Appendix at the back of this workbook is a "Relapse Prevention Quiz." Take it and have your therapist go over it with you. You can also give the test to your family. It's a good review.

Keep in mind that you have many choices ahead of you. You have the power to make decisions with either positive or negative consequences for you and for others. The more you increase your self-understanding, understanding of others, communication and social skills, and think clearly and positively, the safer you will be from reoffenses and the happier you will be in general. And engrave the words *Avoidance* and *Escape* permanently in your memory. They can help you out of all kinds of dangerous situations.

APPENDIX

RELAPSE PREVENTION QUIZ

1) *Relapse Prevention* includes developing alternative thoughts and behaviors that will keep you safe from reoffense at each step of your offense chain. Fill in the steps of your chain, and how you will think and behave differently.

Step	*Your Offense Chain*	*Different Thoughts*	*Other Behaviors*
Seemingly	__________	__________	__________
Unimportant	__________	__________	__________
Decision	__________	__________	__________
High Risk	__________	__________	__________
Situation	__________	__________	__________
Lapse:	__________	__________	__________
(Fantasy or	__________	__________	__________
Dangerous Act)	__________	__________	__________
Giving Up	__________	__________	__________
(What the heck,	__________	__________	__________
why not?)	__________	__________	__________
Reoffense		(too late)	

2) Why do most sex offenders commit sex offenses? What are they looking for? (List at least 3 things.) ________

____

____

____

____

____

3) What are some alternative ways to satisfy each of these needs? (Healthier choices) ____________

____

____

____

____

____

4) What are some ways many sexual abuse victims feel? (List at least three.) ________________

5) List four ways you can best express your anger and frustration.________________

6) List three people you can talk to about your offense and about offending. ________________

7 What are three healthy things to do if you feel depressed or anxious? ________________

8) Why are victims of exposers and obscene phone callers usually frightened and upset? ________________

9) Why do some victims keep silent and cooperate during the sexual offense? ________________

10) Is it true that if a man has an erection, he has to have sex? What happens if he doesn't have sex? Is this the same or different from other bodily urges? ______

11) Why would it be good for you to eliminate the word "can't" from your vocabulary? What word or phrase could you use instead? ______

12) Why is it important to communicate feelings and thoughts to other people? ______

13) What shouldn't you use sex for? (List at least three unhealthy uses of sex.) ______

14) How are you going to avoid getting into the same trouble again? ______

RECOMMENDED READING

Young, Gay and Proud, edited by Sasha Alyson (1985). Alyson Publications, P.O. Box 2783 Dept. B-1, Boston, MA 12208.

Beginning to Heal, by Ellen Bass and Laura Davis (1993). HarperCollins. Also, **The Courage to Heal Workbook,** by Laura Davis (1990). Harper & Row, NY.

Macho: Is That What I Really Want? by Py Bateman and Bill Mahoney (1986). Youth Education Systems, Box 223, Scarborough, NY 10510.

Changing Bodies, Changing Lives: A Book for Teens about Sex and Relationships, by Ruth Bell (1988). Random House, NY.

Repeat After Me, by Claudia Black (1985). M.A.C. Printing and Publications, Denver, CO.

Top Secret – Sexual Assault Information for Teenagers Only, by Jennifer Fay and Billie Jo Flerchinger (1985). Network Publications, P.O. Box 8506, Santa Cruz, CA 95061.

A Guide for Parents of Young Sex Offenders, by Eliana Gil (1987). Launch Press, P.O. Box 5629, Rockville, MD 20855

Outgrowing the Pain: A Book for and about Adults Abused as Children, by Eliana Gil (1988). Launch Press, P.O. Box 5629, Rockville, MD 20855

The Staying Sober Workbook, by Terence T. Gorski (1988). Independence Press, P.O. Box HH, 3225 S. Noland Road, Independence, MO 64055.

One Teenager in 10: Writings by Gay and Lesbian Youth, edited by Ann Heron (1983). Alyson Publications, P.O. Box 2783 Dept. B-1, Boston, MA.

The Cognitive Therapy Workbook, by Rob L. Herrington (1987). CTR, P.O. Box 203332, San Diego, California 92120.

Victims No Longer: Men Recovering from Incest and Other Sexual Child Abuse, by M. Lew. (1988). Harper & Row, NY.

The Teenage Body Book, by Kathy McCoy and Charles Wibbelsman (1983). Pocket Books, A Division of Simon and Schuster, 1230 Avenue of the Americas, New York, NY 10020.

Secret Feelings and Thoughts, by Rosemary Narimanian (1991). Philly Kids Play It Safe, 1600 Arch St. 8th Fl, Philadelphia, PA 19103.

For Guys My Age: A Book about Sexual Abuse for Young Men, by Matthew Taylor (1990). Hawthorne Center, 1847 Haggerty Road, Northville, MI 48161.

SELECTED SAFER SOCIETY PUBLICATIONS

Pathways: A Guided Workbook for Youth Beginning Treatment, by Timothy J. Kahn (2001). Also, **Pathways Guide for Parents of Youth Beginning Treatment,** by Timothy J. Kahn (2002).

Man-to-man: When Your Partner Says No, by Scott Allen Johnson (1992).

Adults Molested as Children: A Survivor's Manual for Women & Men, by Euan Bear with Peter Dimock (1988).

Family Fallout: A Handbook for Families of Adult Sexual Abuse Survivors, by Dorothy Beaulien Landry (1991).

From Trauma to Understanding: A Guide for Parents of Children with Sexual Behavior Problems, by William D. Pithers, Alison S. Gray, Carolyn Cunningham, and Sandy Lane (1993).

Roadmaps to Recovery: A Guided Workbook for Young People in Treatment, by Timothy J. Kahn (1999).

Tell It Like It Is: A Resource Guide for Youth in Treatment, by Alice Tallmadge with Gaylyn Forster (1998).

Adult Relapse Prevenion Workbook, by Charleen Steen (2001).